Other works by the same author

How to Make ESP Work for You
How to Solve Mysteries of Your Mind and Soul
Your Key to Happiness
Know Your Own Mind
You Live After Death
How to Use the Power of Prayer
Thoughts Through Space, with Hubert Wilkins
Anyone Can Stop Drinking
Adventures in Thinking

THE NEW TNT—
MIRACULOUS POWER
WITHIN YOU

Harold Sherman

A Fireside Book
Published by Simon & Schuster, Inc.
New York

Copyright © 1966 by Prentice Hall, Inc.

All rights reserved including the right of reproduction in whole or in part
in any form

The Fireside Edition, 1986
Published by Simon & Schuster, Inc.

Simon & Schuster Building
Rockefeller Center
1230 Avenue of the Americas
New York, New York 10020

Published by arrangement with Prentice-Hall, Inc.

FIRESIDE and colophon are registered trademarks of Simon & Schuster, Inc.

Manufactured in the United States of America

    2   3   4   5   6   7   8   9   10

Library of Congress Cataloging in Publication Data

ISBN 0-671-62428-8

Foreword

The book you now hold in your hands is ready to explode any minute in your mind. Like its predecessor, *TNT— The Power Within You,* which changed the thinking and the lives of several million men and women, it not only contains more DYNAMITE in verbal form—it contains even more KNOWLEDGE of Self which can and will, as you apply it, take you from where you are to where you want to be!

What's TNT?

It stands for POWER—a God-given *creative power* of mind. POWER which all inventors, scientists, physicists, biologists, chemists, astronomers, engineers, electronic experts, space technicians, astronauts, architects, doctors, psychiatrists, business executives, clerks, workers—men and women in all walks of life, *yourself included*—possess in varying degrees of development!

All successful people have drawn upon this POWER, knowingly or unknowingly, to achieve their success, because success cannot be attained without it.

Harold Sherman, author of this new, revised edition of TNT, also authored *TNT—The Power Within You,* which he based on an inspirational booklet that Claude Bristol, author of *The Magic of Believing,* had written some twenty years before, and titled: *TNT—It Rocks the Earth.* Following Mr. Bristol's death in 1951, Prentice-Hall, Inc. arranged with Mr. Sherman who shared Bristol's philosophy, to expand his booklet into book length. *TNT—The Power Within You* thus bore the names of Bristol and Sherman as co-authors. It became one of the all-time best sellers in the self-help field.

And now, Harold Sherman has created this sequel, *The New TNT—Miraculous Power Within You,* which is even more exciting and inspiring.

The New TNT takes up where *TNT—The Power Within You* left off, reinforcing its proven techniques of right thinking with new case histories and considerable new material. Herein you will find abundant evidence that what you PICTURE in your mind, supported by the necessary EFFORT and FAITH, can, one day, become an accomplished fact in *your* life!

Contents

THE NEW TNT—
MIRACULOUS POWER
WITHIN YOU

1

Your Changing
Outer and Inner Worlds

In 1954, when *TNT—The Power Within You* first exploded in the consciousness of men and women readers, it blasted old, false concepts and fixed ideas of fear and worry and wrong thinking from many minds and put these individuals on the road to new opportunities and accomplishments.

Since that time I have received and continue to receive grateful letters and testimonials of achievement from hundreds—yes, thousands—of *TNT* readers who tell me, in essence:

"It *works!* Once I learned how to draw upon these wonderful creative powers of mind, I began to get results. Began to leave my former problems and difficulties and frustrations behind. Began to attain better health, more self-confidence, a more positive, cheerful, optimistic attitude toward life, a better understanding of myself and others—in short, greater happiness in every aspect of my personal and social and business life!"

NOW, after these first ten years—in answer to increasing requests for MORE information about *TNT—The Power Within You*—I present to you this new, revised volume, combining the tested and proved techniques of the original, with new case history reports and added self-knowledge—to

1

aid earlier as well as new readers in getting from where they are to where they want to be!

If you have already been exposed to *TNT*, you are not where you were prior to that exposure. I say this with positive assurance because I defy you or anyone to read and apply this knowledge without getting a "booster shot" that will lift you higher in life than you have been before. It is impossible to start thinking right and to continue to get wrong results!

Thirty to fifty years ago, this knowledge of self wasn't available in too understandable and applicable a form. You had to dig for it on a trial-and-error basis. The ancients had tried to tell us that, "As a man thinketh in his mind and heart, so is he!" But, while it sounded nice, it still seemed a little Sunday-schoolish when confronted by everyday problems and situations.

That was before we began to realize the great and infallible power of thought—that man has risen to his present place on this earth and is now preparing to take off for distant planets solely on the wings of his *thoughts!* Compared with atomic power, a force discovered and developed by man's mind, THOUGHT towers toward Infinity! Just as there appears to be no limit to the ever expanding physical universe, there is demonstrably no limit to the ever expanding creativity of the human mind! What man can picture in his mind, he can, one day, achieve. And, we can more readily understand and apply the oft-quoted statement of the ancients, by declaring:

"As a man PICTURES in his mind and in his heart—so is he!"

ALL CHANGES DUE TO THOUGHT

In the last ten years, *you* have changed considerably.
So have I!

You are changing right now as you read this sentence.
So am I!

So is everything in the entire Universe because nothing is standing still. Nothing is exactly the same as it was, even a split second ago.

Something has been happening to you, both outside and inside your body and your mind, from the moment you were born, and these happenings have left their influence upon you—molding you inexorably into the individual you are today!

This is the way life is. It compels you to keep moving, either forward or backward—depending on what you decide to do and how you decide to do it.

WHICH WAY ARE YOU GOING?

There is only one question you should ask yourself: "Am I headed in the right direction?"

If you are going backward—if you feel you have been slipping in the race of life, if you are not attaining what you started out to achieve, there is but one answer you should make to yourself. You should stand up before a mirror, or see yourself in your mind's eye, and tell yourself in no uncertain terms:

"The time has come for you to reverse directions! Get on the right *mental track!* Switch all your wrong thinking off the main line—and clear it for action! You have wasted enough time on self-pity and blaming others and circumstances seemingly beyond control for all things that have gone wrong—for the obstacles in your path. From now on, you are leaving all this excess baggage behind. You are freeing your mind of all past grievances and resentments. You are starting all over with new thoughts and new ideas and new resolution—and the faith that, as you change your thinking, great and good changes are going to come into your life!"

Feel better? Sure, you do! It's given me a lift every time I've faced myself and told myself the truth about myself. Oh, of course, the truth has hurt, lots of times. But, as I've often said, "I'd much rather hurt myself than let others hurt me!"

If I can discover my faults and weaknesses and start to work on them before someone else reminds me of them in a most unpleasant way, or before they get me into trouble— I figure I've taken the easiest and best way out.

You may have needed to give yourself a good talking to, for some time. It is the simplest thing in the world to get into a mental rut. To feel sorry for yourself, disgusted with life and people, ready to give up on a project or ambition. These feelings are common to all of us—even to those whom you look upon as successful men and women. They have their tests, their disappointments and disillusionments, too.

YOUR TIME FOR PERSONAL INVENTORY

Today is the only time you have. This minute is yours to do with as you will, as long as it exists. And then you are into the next minute, and the next, and if you are not spending your time profitably, it is slipping away from you forever.

A great man once said: "If I only had again the time I have lost doing nothing worthwhile, how much more I could have accomplished!"

Time is going faster today because, in this changing world, you have to divide up Time between so many things you want to do or feel compelled to do. There are so many interests and activities inviting your participation that it is difficult to choose among them and you may end up getting so involved that you cannot give adequate attention to any. If so, this may call for a streamlining of your daily operations so you can free Time to concentrate upon what means most to you and your loved ones.

If you find yourself saying, "I haven't time to do what I should be doing, or want to do," then you can never hope to realize tomorrow what you desire today.

Any change in your thinking starts now. Can you, will you take the time, *make* the time, to devote a few minutes a day, to clearing your mental deck for ACTION?

Will you begin by taking a personal inventory of yourself? Asking yourself frank questions and demanding frank answers?

You actually know yourself better than anyone else can know you. But you may not like to admit, at first, some of the things you will uncover about yourself.

For example:

> *How do you stack up in today's world?*
> *Are you happy in it?*
>
> *How do you get along with others?*
>
> *Do you have ambitions to go places beyond your present situation in life?*
>
> *Do you have money problems?*
>
> *How are your personal habits?*
>
> *Do you have marital problems?*
>
> *Are you alone and lonely?*
>
> *How do you rate your personality and physical appearance?*
>
> *Do you need a better educational background?*
>
> *Are you keeping pace with the rapid social and economic changes?*

These are just a few of the questions you need to ask yourself in determining how you stand in today's world—and if you are not satisfied with some of the answers you get—perhaps what I have to say in this book will help take you from where you are to where you want to be.

But I would be doing you a disservice by not pointing this out at the very start. You will not find what I present in these pages to be a "pie-in-the-sky" philosophy, one that invites you to put your "mental head" in the sand and to try to create the kind of a world you want with nice-sounding platitudes and affirmations.

This wonderful and yet still mysterious creative power of mind does not respond to these intellectual exercises. It is your *deep feeling* that generates the power behind thought. What you *really want,* or what you *fear,* activates this power, causing it to magnetize, so to speak, conditions around you, and to start attracting what is required in the way of experiences and events, to produce what you have visualized.

You have heard this before, but it is worth repeating: "*Like attracts like in the realm of mind!*" This is a universal law—the law of cause and effect. It functions automatically, everlastingly, and plays no favorites. Woe be unto you if you don't pay heed to this law! It means that hate attracts hate, and prejudice attracts prejudice—and so on and on! This explains, to a great degree, the turbulent conditions in today's world. Great populations of people who are disturbed mentally, emotionally and physically materialize these disturbances in the form of protests and riots and bombings, and killings and all manner of violent acts, leading eventually to war. All past history is tragic proof of this.

You are a part of humanity, regardless of your race or color or where you live or what you do. On every side you are witness to the unhappy consequences of man's wrong thinking. Many men and women are turning the marvelous God-given creative powers of mind against themselves and against their fellow humans!

They are not doing this willfully, so much as ignorantly. The majority of them have not yet connected their destructive mental and emotional attitudes with the destructive things that are happening to them and to others. When they do, they will realize that THOUGHT, and thought alone, has produced these conditions.

Here it is—in capsule form:

What you put into your mind in the nature of your thoughts and feelings (desires or fears) is what subsequently materializes for you in your outer world. You should therefore accept this basic fact—as your thoughts change, the events in your outer world change! Which is another way of saying that *things first happen in the mind before they can and do happen in your external life.*

To illustrate: you cannot so much as lay this book aside until you give a mental command for your hands to perform the act.

GREAT POWERS OF MIND STILL LITTLE KNOWN

With all the use man has made of his mind, he still knows little about the deeper aspects of it. But he is beginning, at last, to delve into the mysterious depths of his own consciousness and to make highly significant discoveries.

As you may know, I have devoted a lifetime to a study of the higher powers of the mind, and I say to you with profound conviction (based upon years of research and personal experimentation) that your mind possesses:

Power to create . . . power to heal . . . power to attract . . . power to repel . . . power to transmit and receive thoughts . . . power to sense conditions and events at a distance . . . power, at times to perceive the future . . . power to derive

7

daily guidance from Higher Sources deep within your subconscious.

But before you can enjoy the full benefit of these powers, you must learn how to control and direct them. They are working for you now, spontaneously and spasmodically. You can recall times when you have had strong urges to do or not to do something, definite feelings that certain things had happened or were going to happen, a sudden dream-like solution of a problem, a guiding flash of intuition—all of which proved out, despite doubts you may have had at the moment.

Most of these occurrences were not happenstance: they were your extrasensory faculties trying to break through the resistance of your conscious mind and be of service to you.

YOU MUST BELIEVE

Of course you cannot impress your "TNT"—this creative power within you—to work successfully for you if you do not believe in it. Your mind is highly sensitive to suggestion. Tell it "you can't do something"—and you can't. Your subconscious doesn't reason or argue with you—it just accepts. But give it an order to get busy on a project, and picture what you want it to do, with real feeling behind it, and the whole creative machinery of your mind starts to work. More than that—as long as you hold this picture, with faith, in your mind, it never lets up until what you have visualized becomes an accomplished fact.

A skeptical person will not achieve comparable results because he lacks faith. But the creative power is functioning in his mind just as it is in anyone else's. Whatever he pictures, good or bad, desiring it or fearing it, is attracted to him in due time, in some form. You cannot keep this creative power from working for or against you, dependent on the nature of your thoughts and feelings. No one can.

8

UNHAPPINESS DUE TO WRONG THINKING

Many people in the world today are unhappy, largely because of their wrong thinking. It is creating trouble among individuals and conditions of turmoil, unrest and open conflict in many communities as well as countries. As a result, mental illness is leading all other illnesses, and heart disease and alcoholism are not far behind. This is testimony to our disturbed reaction to the things that are happening to us, the pace we are living, the pressures we are under, the mental and physical strains we are experiencing.

In this Space Age, there is fear of the future; feelings of uncertainty and insecurity are widespread. Will there be a third World War? What is automation going to do to us? Are we headed for another economic depression? Can all races and colors of people ever live peacefully together? How are our children going to make out? Are we safe on the streets and on the highways or even in our own homes any more? Why are people getting more lawless in their conduct, more careless of life and property? Is there really a God, a Supreme Being, a Great Intelligence that has any personal concern for creature man?

These vital questions and many more are beating into the consciousness of men and women throughout the world. They are leading to a revolution in thought. People aren't thinking and acting and reacting the way they did a few years ago—and there is never going to be a return to the "good old days." No matter how much you may desire it, you can't run away from changing world conditions. They will catch up with you, eventually, wherever you are, and you will be affected, in some manner, by them.

GOOD AND BAD IN EVERYTHING

You are in the presence of constantly unfolding wonders as Science leads you further and further into the Space Age.

But these awesome, yet promising, new developments also bring with them great dangers and terrific problems. This is because, in the world of nature as well as in the world of man, there is nothing good that does not have its bad side.

Atomic power, as you know, can incinerate the earth, and it can also, in time, liberate man from all drudgery. Take man to the moon and distant planets. Convert the oceans' salt water into fresh water, irrigate vast barren wastes, provide living conditions for millions now starving, supply the energy to meet the industrial needs of every nation—and give man the freedom, at last, to develop himself, in knowledge and character.

But—will he do it? He MUST—if he is to survive!

In order to live happily and successfully and with the assurance of a reasonable degree of safety and security in today's disturbed world, your greatest, your only, fundamental protection is your maintenance of the right mental attitude—your ability to remain calm and composed and clear minded under stressful conditions which might otherwise completely upset you mentally, emotionally and physically.

This is the theme of this book: how you and I can prepare ourselves, mentally and spiritually, to live in this changing world! It's not going to be easy because we are going to be tested, in one way or another, every day of our lives.

One day it could be an argument with a neighbor, a misunderstanding with a friend, an auto accident, loss of a job, an emotional upset between husband or wife, trouble with an unruly or wayward child, disillusionment over a business deal or business associate, difficulty over money matters, a developing racial problem, ill feeling between relatives or in-laws, concern over the health of a friend or loved one, worry over world conditions, a son or daughter away from home or in service, your own state of health—*you name it!*

Any of these conditions, and countless more, can have a

devastating effect upon you—unless you possess the developed ability to meet them while maintaining control of your mind and emotions.

YOU MUST DEAL WITH OTHER MINDS

In this changing world, you not only have to be responsible for your own thoughts and feelings—you must, at the same time, protect yourself against the negative or combative thoughts and feelings of others.

General Thomas E. Powers, former head of the Strategic Air Command, has said: "Man is not a peaceful animal."

My grandmother, Mary E. Morrow, was a remarkable woman who possessed a deep and abiding faith in the higher powers of the mind, and in God. She faced many tribulations with great and quiet stoicism. Found among her papers, after she passed on at an advanced age, were the following penned thoughts, which I have often recalled when the going has seemed rough:

> *"We all have a work to do. . . . A goal in life . . . and we cannot expect to reach it without a sometimes bloody battle."*

Life does not have to be bloody, but it can be rugged at times because each day brings us new experiences and new associations with different types of people, with which and with whom we must deal.

We cannot expect everyone to be in agreement with us on various issues that may arise, nor can we expect everyone to be honest and aboveboard in his or her relations. Yet I have found that, under any ordinary circumstances, if you are decent in your treatment of others that they, nine times out of ten, will be decent in their treatment of you. Again, the law of "like attracting like" in operation.

Nevertheless, human nature being what it is, you will

11

encounter some individuals with whom it will be difficult if not impossible to get along. You doubtless have run into such persons long before this. In these cases, it is better to to get along, if you can, without them.

There will be those who will try to dominate your life, to control your thoughts and acts, if you let them. Your most priceless possession is your own freedom of choice, of decision, of action.

This is the time, should you be under the influence of someone else, to declare your independence. If it concerns a loved one or close friend, do it diplomatically but firmly. You cannot direct your own life while it is under the direction of another. You can work harmoniously with others, serving them voluntarily, through love, obligation or a sense of duty—but not to be free to express your own thoughts and feelings or pursue your own rightful interests and desires in life is enslavement.

GET READY TO PICTURE A BRIGHTER FUTURE!

Decide now to take definite steps toward a better future— to think new thoughts, to invite new ideas, to attract new and finer experiences!

You can, to a greater extent than you at present realize, take control of your own destiny.

Reduced to utter simplicity, your basic happiness depends largely upon what you think of others and what they think of you. On how you react to what happens to you; on how free your mind is of any possible fears or hates or prejudices, or feelings of inferiority or insecurity, and the like; of whether or not you enjoy what you are doing and the people with whom you are working, or with whom you are associated; of whether you find it pleasant to live with yourself; of whether or not you and your loved ones are getting along; of whether your conditions in your home life are what they ought to be.

This is all an essential part of living—and if one or more of these things is not right, you have some *corrective* mental picturing to do!

Remember—you can't change your conditions in life until and unless you change your *thinking!*

THOUGHTS TO BUILD INTO YOUR LIFE

What I can picture in my mind, I can one day achieve.

Today is the only time I have. Therefore, I will fill it with satisfying and constructive activities.

Nothing can contribute more vitally to my own progress than the daily attempt to discover and remove my own faults and weaknesses.

I will always remember that any change in my life starts with a change in my thinking, because "like always attracts like" in the realm of mind.

To live happily and successfully I must maintain the right mental attitude—the ability to remain calm and composed and clear-minded under any and all conditions.

2

Start by Analyzing Yourself

You are the result today of all your PAST thinking.

Every EXPERIENCE you have had is recorded in your MIND and continues to exist in MEMORY, whether you can recall it at will or not.

The GOOD thoughts and happenings, with the BAD!

It is a universal law that LIKE attracts LIKE!

Therefore, GOOD thoughts attract GOOD happenings; BAD thoughts attract BAD happenings.

Let's examine your LIFETIME thoughts and discover WHY certain things have happened to you—and other things have not!

WHY you may have had experiences you thought you DIDN'T want, and WHY many things you thought you DID want never came to pass!

Are you ready to discover your weak points and find out what you need to "work on" to improve your own personality, thinking and conditions in life?

If you are, then prepare to ASK YOURSELF THESE FRANK PERSONAL QUESTIONS. Upon your answers will be determined your need for self-development!

Do you know HOW your MIND *really* operates?

Do you know that you think in MENTAL PICTURES and that if you PICTURE something in your MIND

14

strongly enough and confidently enough, it may ultimately come to pass? (Either for your GOOD or BAD, depending upon the NATURE of your MENTAL PICTURES!)

This being true, what kind of PICTURES are you carrying in your MIND today?

Get a separate sheet of paper or notebook and write down what you THINK and how you FEEL about—

1. Your Closest Friend (Sweetheart or Relation)
2. Your Wife or Husband (If married)
3. Your Children (Love, resent or hate them?)
4. Your Boss (If employed)
5. Your Work (Enjoy or detest it?)
6. Your Position in Life (Beneath you? Too hard to maintain?)
7. Your Religion (Is it comforting, helpful, inspiring?)
8. Your Religious Conviction (Do you really believe?)
9. Your Tolerance (Do you respect beliefs of others?)
10. Your Faith in Yourself (Can you stand alone in crisis?)
11. Your Hates and Prejudices (What are they? Why?)
12. Your Spare-time Activities (Beneficial? Time-killing?)
13. Your Fears and Worries (List them all)
14. Your Sex Urges (Are they being satisfied?)
15. Your Health (Is it what it should be?)
16. Your Physical Exercise (Not enough or too much?)
17. Your Habits (Are you master of them?)
18. Your Goal in Life (Do you have any? Is it worthwhile?)
19. Your Appearance (Can it be improved?)
20. Your Personality (Attractive? Can it be more so?)
21. Your Temperament (Carefree? Too serious? Tense? Emotional?)
22. Your Sense of Humor (Enough? Need to be cultivated?)
23. Your Mental Attitude (Positive or negative, mostly?)

15

24. Your Disposition (Cheery? Depressed?)
25. Your Ego (Self-centered? Interested in others?)
26. Your Pride (Like flattery or honest opinions?)
27. Your Self-respect (Will you fight to preserve it?)
28. Your Love of Principle (Strong or weak?)
29. Your Sense of Loyalty (Do you demand and give it?)
30. Your Concentration (Can you think under pressure?)
31. Your Ability to Relax (Can you let go instantly?)
32. Your Persistence (Give up easily? Never quit?)
33. Your Unbidden Thoughts (Repressed desires? Fears?)
34. Your Family Life (Pleasant? Get on your nerves?)
35. Your Complexes (Fixation on father, mother, brother, sister?)
36. Your Punctuality (Do you keep others waiting?)
37. Your Point of View (Do you try to see the other fellow's?)
38. Your Memory (Things you want to forget? Why?)
39. Your Self-expression (Easy or difficult? Why?)
40. Your Self-confidence (Feel inferior? Incapable? Why?)

Your ANSWER to these questions should give you a fairly accurate PICTURE of yourself as you are TODAY!

But ALL that is happening to you NOW had its beginnings somewhere in your YESTERDAYS, perhaps even back in your EARLY CHILDHOOD. For this reason—if you are to enjoy GREATER HAPPINESS through overcoming PRESENT conditions and obstacles—you must review your PAST experiences and ROOT OUT all WRONG THOUGHTS and EMOTIONAL REACTIONS. As you do so, you will clearly see the EFFECT that UNCORRECTED mental pictures are having upon your PRESENT LIFE.

So now, get set and ask yourself what kind of PICTURES have you carried in MIND in the PAST?

16

Once again, record these answers frankly and honestly on a separate sheet of paper or notebook, writing down what your THOUGHTS and FEELINGS have been.

1. What is your earliest childhood recollection? (Is it about your mother, a fall, a burn? Describe in full.)
2. Were you jealous of either parent? (Do you know why?)
3. Was your mother or father affectionate? (Not enough? Too much so?)
4. Whom did you like best—father or mother? (Why?)
5. Do you think you developed a father or mother complex?
6. Was it emotionally difficult for you to leave home?
7. Do you feel independent of parental influence now?
8. Do you still feel parental judgment to be best? (Rely or lean on it?)
9. Could you talk freely with parents on all subjects? (Or repressed?)
10. Do you feel that parents understood you? (Only one—or neither?)
11. Were you permitted to play with all children? (If not, why not?)
12. Did parents have racial or religious prejudices? (And pass them on?)
13. Was religion a part of home life? (Did you like it or resent it?)
14. Did you have early sex experiences? (Own making? Suggested by others?)
15. Were your first concepts of sex clean or vulgar?
16. Have you been left with unnatural or repressed desires?
17. Are these desires disturbing your sex happiness today?
18. Do you have deep feelings of "guilt" for past sex offenses?

19. Have you suffered from a parental fixation which has upset sex life?
20. Did your father or mother oppose your marrying, leaving home?
21. Does either interfere with your home life now?
22. When a child were you always spared hard work?
23. Were you taught to finish each job, once started?
24. Did you go to parents for comfort and aid when things went wrong?
25. Were you babied and put to bed each time you felt bad?
26. Could your parents see the funny side of things? (Or too serious?)
27. Were you taught that doing things could be interesting and a pleasure, as well as work?
28. Were you encouraged to try again if you did not succeed the first time?
29. Were you favored over other members of family or did you feel yourself neglected?
30. Were you on time at school? Did you respect time of others?
31. Were you orderly and neat about personal habits?
32. Did you feel that your parents really wanted and loved you?
33. Were you permitted to express yourself or were you repressed, your opinions not treated seriously?
34. Did you belong to clubs, organizations and groups in school?
35. Were you shy, backward, self-conscious?
36. Were you sensitive to criticism?
37. Did you hate either parent? Why?
38. Did you fear the dark? Ever locked in dark place as punishment?
39. Were you compared unfavorably to others?

40. Have you developed fears of punishment, fears of misconduct, fears of things going wrong?

These questions and your answers are sufficient to reveal to you STATES of MIND and EMOTIONAL REACTIONS that you need to change for your own good.

This analysis of SELF, when you have completed and studied it, *impersonally* and *objectively*, should PROVE to you the EFFECT of THOUGHT on your LIFE, and its POWER to bring you HAPPINESS or SORROW, SUCCESS or FAILURE.

Armed with this knowledge of your strengths and weaknesses, you are now ready to start on the PATH of SELF-DEVELOPMENT, which can enable you to overcome many WRONG MENTAL ATTITUDES and begin to attain, through RIGHT VISUALIZATION, the happiness and success you have always desired.

Keep this ANALYSIS you have made of yourself ABSOLUTELY PRIVATE, and check it against your own development as you begin to IMPROVE your condition in life through RIGHT THINKING.

You will be amazed and delighted at the PROGRESS you can make. This can be the greatest TURNING POINT in your life, as it has been for thousands upon thousands of other men and women throughout the world. They have regained health, happiness, prosperity—all the GOOD things of life—by learning and applying these same SIMPLE TECHNIQUES OF RIGHT THINKING.

THOUGHTS TO BUILD INTO YOUR LIFE

I realize that I am the result today of all my past thinking . . .

That all that is happening to me now had its beginning in my yesterdays . . .

19

That I think, basically, in mental pictures . . .

That what I picture vividly and confidently and steadfastly in my mind becomes the blueprint that the Creative Power in my Subconscious goes to work on . . .

That what I picture myself doing or being or having—believing it will one day come to pass, will eventually cause what I desire to materialize in my outer life!

3

The Power of Picturing
What You Want!

When I first realized that I was attracting unhappy experiences to myself by the kind of thoughts I was thinking, it really rocked me. Up to that time, I, like many others, had been blaming the other fellow and outside forces and conditions for the mess I was in. I just knew I hadn't been responsible for what had been happening to me, and it helped salve my many hurts to pretend I hadn't been to blame. But, deep down within, I had begun to wonder if the way I thought and felt about things didn't have some connection!

If I got up in the morning, depressed and convinced it was going to be a bad day, it more often than not turned out to be a bad day. At first I thought I was "psychic," that I could tell in advance what was going to happen. It took a long time, and I absorbed a lot of unnecessary punishment before I discovered, as I have already mentioned, that "like always attracts like" in the realm of mind, and that I had been creating what happened to me by wrong thinking.

Looking around me, I saw happy men and women to whom happy things were happening. They got up in the morning expecting good things to come to them—and good things did!

Sometimes these happy people had unhappy experiences,

21

but I noticed that they didn't let these experiences get them down. They rose the next day expecting *more* good things to happen, and sure enough *more* good things did!

Before my awakening came, this always amazed me. I even resented it. Why should just a different mental attitude make so much difference?

I didn't know then that in the world there is a mighty force which scientists call electromagnetism. I didn't know that everything in the universe is electromagnetic in nature, that the laws of attraction and repulsion operate electromagnetically; that when you assume a positive or negative attitude of mind, you get a positive or negative result; that there is no such thing as an accident in life—that everything happens in direct accordance with *the laws of cause and effect!*

Read and reread the foregoing paragraph! Let these facts soak in till you never forget them, because they have the power to change your life!

There is nothing new in what I am telling you, except as it may be new to you. This same message has been written and delivered thousands of times.

The wisest men of all ages, the "medicine men," religious leaders, great teachers, the Mayan priests, the Yogis, healers and miracle men—all of them knew this secret. Some worked it one way, some another.

They pictured in their minds and hearts what they wanted —and what they pictured eventually came true!

Moses *pictured* leading his people to the Promised Land; Alexander the Great and Napoleon *pictured* great conquests; Shakespeare *pictured* the creation of his immortal writings; Washington *pictured* the winning of independence for the Thirteen Colonies; Lincoln *pictured* the freeing of the slaves and the preservation of the Union; Benjamin Franklin *pictured* the capture of lightning through a

22

kite as a means of proving that electricity and lightning are the same force; Edison *pictured* the electric light, motion picture, the phonograph, the electric train and countless other great inventions; Steinmetz *pictured* new uses for electric power; Barnum *pictured* "the greatest show on earth"—a circus that would travel around the world by train; Roosevelt *pictured* leading his country out of its worst depression; Eisenhower *pictured* leading the Allied Armies to a World War II victory over Germany and Japan; Einstein *pictured* development of a formula that would explain the functioning of the basic forces in the Universe; Churchill *pictured* England surviving its "darkest hour" and projected this picture to the minds and hearts of all his countrymen so powerfully and so vividly that they stood off the most savage and devastating attacks of all history, to save the free world.

These were great pictures by great and inspired men, and all these pictures, held resolutely in mind and converted into action, were brought to pass by the faith and energy and vision and courage and steadfastness of each individual.

These men, and many like them, were just human beings like yourself. If they knew and could achieve, so can you.

HALT! THINK! PONDER!

What made these people great? It was that they pictured themselves attaining! They dared to picture great achievement. And the power within, given these pictures to work on, finally brought them into being.

You have to *think* big to *be* big. A small man is made up of small thoughts. He cannot remain small and think BIG!

REFLECT FOR A MOMENT!

Where did the steamboat, the locomotive, the automobile, the electric light, the typewriter, the sewing machine, the airplane, the radio, television, spaceships and a million other objects and conveniences come from? All were thoughts or mental pictures in the minds of men before these things became realities. Everything on this earth, except that which nature creates or has provided, is the result of sustained thought.

Take out of this world everything that has been created by thought alone, and you would have nothing left but the primitive jungle. This is the quickest, most graphic way to give you a comprehension of what the mind of man has done.

When the real history of the evolution of mind is written, it will be the greatest, most thrilling story of all time, because it will cover all time and every phase of human experience.

This story will tell how man required thousands upon thousands of years to emerge from the depths of ignorance, superstition, fear, prejudice, mythology and wrong concepts.

It will tell of great thinkers like Galileo, who believed, like Copernicus, that the earth moves around the sun—he was compelled by the Inquisition to recant his statements and was forbidden to publish his learned books. With what shame we look back upon such persecutions by the early Church of men who dared pursue the Truth despite existing doctrines and decrees.

The history of the human mind will give honor to Charles Darwin, whose profound study of plants and animals led to his famous, world-shaking *The Origin of Species,* in which he advanced the theory of evolution. To the credit of modern theology, God's handiwork in and through evolution is now being recognized by many religious sects.

Time's majestic march through the ages has seen man's mind develop powers he little dreamed of during his early days on earth.

PROOF THAT MAN IS MORE THAN ANIMAL

The fact that creature man has been able to survive throughout the centuries in the struggle against all forms of life, and in spite of the inhumanities to his fellow man, is proof that he possesses superior powers within. Man is a veritable god in the making, although he reveals, still too often, devilish tendencies.

It is the inner power that man possesses, beyond and apart from any other living creature on this earth, which has made it possible for him to advance to his present state of development and awareness.

The power within has lifted man above all other animals. While there may be higher intelligence on other planets and in higher realms of being, it is now evident that man has unlimited potentialities for further development within himself. He is just in the kindergarten of his opportunities for unfoldment and achievement; these will come to fruition once he learns how to live peacefully and co-operatively with his fellow man. He is in the midst of learning this painful lesson now. But I have faith he is going to learn it. I have faith in this vast inner power, greater than man, of which he is becoming more and more conscious—"that something" which can and will eventually free him from his fears and hates and prejudices, giving him such understanding of himself that he will, in turn, be able to understand others.

You always know when a man or woman is using the power within his or her life. Such people walk in the consciousness of this power, which is in and behind their every thought and act. They are poised, self-assured, courageous, uninhibited and magnetic in expression. They know where they are going and how to get there. They have pictured their futures and are moving with resoluteness and conviction into them. There is a contagious spirit about them.

They tend to carry you along with them, to spur you on to greater efforts in your own behalf. These people are the *planners* and the *doers* of the world. The great mass of unthinking human beings follow in their wake.

Do you lead the pack, or are you one of the pack? If you are a follower of others, you have not yet discovered "that something" within you. To be a leader, to be able to step out ahead of the pack in your line of work or human interest or expression, you must know how to draw upon the power within. It is absolutely essential. You cannot do anything without it.

The law of attraction will only bring to you what you *picture*. The creative power within must be *magnetized* by what you visualize for it to do.

PICTURE! PICTURE! PICTURE!

This is the simple command which leads to attainment. *Picture! Picture! Picture!* But be sure you are picturing what you *really* want and not developing pictures of fear and worry, which will cause that inner power to create for you what you *don't* want!

What you picture must come to pass if you picture it long enough, clearly enough and confidently enough. I am going to repeat many of these statements again and again, in different ways, because I want them to be indelibly impressed upon your consciousness.

The successful men and women of the world never lose sight of their *pictures*. They keep on reminding their creative power of what they desire in life, so that it will keep on attracting everything they need to materialize what they have pictured.

EXAMPLE OF PICTURE POWER

Some years ago in New York I met a personable young man by the name of Bob. He told me he was ambitious to go to Hollywood, to seek a career in radio and motion pictures. "But," he said, "I have little money and no connections. Under these circumstances, do you think it foolish for me to go west?"

I said: "Bob—let me ask you one question. 'Do you have faith in yourself and the power of TNT within you?' "

He smiled and replied: "I sure do. That's ALL I've got."

My answer to him was: "If you've got that—and if you picture what you want and are willing to put forth the effort to get it, that's all you need."

Bob hitchhiked to Hollywood. He arrived with eight dollars in his pocket, made the rounds of radio and picture studios, but everywhere received the usual Hollywood answer: "Sorry, you don't have sufficient experience or reputation."

But he kept on picturing himself getting a foothold somewhere, somehow—taking any kind of a job to get in the business. He was confident, if he could just make a connection, that he could prove himself, demonstrate his ability.

Still the opportunity didn't come, so Bob got off by himself one night and reviewed his situation. To be able to stick it out, he needed to find some way to make money. He asked himself what he had ever done in his life that he might now capitalize upon? Had he any past experience that could be turned into money? Bob gave this problem to his creative power of mind and decided to sleep on it. He gave himself the suggestion that he would awaken in the morning with an idea that might be of service.

When morning came, the idea was there! He was taken back in memory to his father's little bake shop in Pennsylvania. He recalled the wonderful pretzels that his father had made—but as he saw these pretzels in his mind's eye, he saw them take the shape of monograms and initials of famous radio and movie stars!

This was IT! A money-making idea! An idea that would

also give him a legitimate reason for personally contacting the biggest people in show business!

Bob lost no time in calling upon the proprietor of a Hollywood bakery. He offered him a proposition: if the baker would make the pretzels up on special order, in the form of monograms and initials of actors, actresses and producers, he, Bob, would visit their homes and offices to make the sales!

The baker went for Bob's ingenious idea, and Bob went to work. It was not long before many Hollywood cocktail parties began to feature pretzels bearing the monograms and initials of great stars. But, as Bob canvassed them personally and they became interested in him, he was able to sell far more than pretzels—he sold himself and his services to some of these stars, joining their production staffs. This led to an offer from the Columbia Broadcasting Company, wherein he was given opportunity to work in different departments and to make a place for himself. It wasn't long before Bob was on the way up as a radio program producer, and he eventually became an agent, representing many star performers.

But, at that time, with his faith in the power of TNT within him firmly established, he began picturing the kind of girl he wanted to marry. Within a few months, he saw the very image of the girl he had in mind—the picture of a beautiful young actress gazed at him from a magazine cover!

He fell in love with this young woman on sight and began picturing himself meeting her and making a good impression. This finally came to pass at a Hollywood party, but Bob was informed, by her escort, that *he* intended to marry her.

This was a shock to Bob, but it didn't change his picture. A while earlier, he had visited a quaint little Mission Church—one hundred and twenty years old—in Palo Alto,

California; the moment he stepped into it he had said: "*This* is where I am going to be married!"

He didn't have *the* girl in mind at that time. He hadn't yet known she existed or seen her picture on the magazine cover. But, after Bob had seen her photograph, he began to picture his wedding to the girl of his dreams, this beautiful young actress who was becoming the talk of Hollywood, and he saw, in his mind's eye, their wedding taking place in the old Mission Church. He saw the two of them, standing side by side, taking their vows. . . .

One day, following their brief meeting at the Hollywood party, Bob dropped in at the Brown Derby restaurant and came upon the girl, breakfasting alone. He knew instantly that the power of TNT was giving him this opportunity to get better acquainted.

As they left the restaurant together, the beautiful young actress stopped before a lending library and looked longingly at a costly set of original copies of Dickens. This gave Bob an idea. It was a few days before Christmas. He bought two secondhand, first-edition copies and sent them to her as a gift.

She phoned to thank him, he made a date—and seven weeks later, they were married in the little old Mission Church—*just as Bob had pictured it!*

Who was the girl? She must remain nameless here because she and Bob desire the identity of their romantic experience to be kept secret. However, you would recognize her name as one of the country's finest stage and screen actresses, could it be mentioned. Today, she and Bob are among Hollywood's happiest married couples. Every word of what has been recounted here is factual.

NOW, have you gained sufficient understanding of the operation of your mind to accept the fact that you will, one day, GET, in one form or another, WHAT you have pictured?

Your power of TNT won't question your order. It will deliver what you desire, or what you fear, without any compunction as to whether it is good or bad for you.

This is for YOU to decide—you are the boss. TNT, the POWER within you, is your SERVANT. It will always do your bidding.

THOUGHTS TO BUILD INTO YOUR LIFE

I recognize and accept the universal fact that everything happens in direct accordance with the laws of Cause and Effect . . .

That I set up definite causes by the kind of thoughts I think, which lead eventually to the production of like effects . . .

That great men and women, throughout all history, have been operating these laws by picturing themselves achieving certain worthwhile objectives. . . .

That these distinguished people, past and present, have made use of the same creative power of mind that I possess . . .

That, by intelligent use of this power, I can accomplish, within reason, whatever I desire to do or be or have in my own life.

4

What Picture
Do Others Have of You?

When you look in the mirror, you only see the external you. This is often almost too revealing. Depending on your age, you see lines and expressions in your face, reflective of experiences you have undergone, or are undergoing, that are showing through.

You cannot long conceal a plaguing fear or worry, a mental or emotional disturbance, a nervous tension of body and mind, a sense of inferiority or inadequacy, a lack of interest or spirit in life, a dislike of others. All these feelings find their way to the surface and are expressed in various thoughts and acts that leave their traces in the way you look, not only to yourself but also to others.

It is difficult enough to find the courage to examine yourself, your faults and weaknesses, but to attempt, at the same time, to "see yourself as others see you," requires just plain intestinal fortitude!

There is no other word for it. None of us wants to get hurt or be hurt, least of all to hurt ourselves, if we can possibly avoid it. But it is sometimes necessary to hurt one's self in order to help one's self and to protect one's self from being hurt even worse. That's where the "guts" come in!

Much depends upon what others think of us—the kind of mental image they have of us. Ordinarily, we don't pay much or any attention to the type of image we create of ourselves—we just go about the business of living, acting and reacting to life's experiences in our association with other people, friends and relatives, letting the "chips," as, they say, fall where they may. But some of these "chips," in the form of our mental attitudes and actions, may trip us up.

I will always regretfully remember a time when, as a young man, I enjoyed matching wits with people I met. At parties or friendly gatherings, if someone said something clever, I would try to say something just a little bit more clever—or funnier. Folks usually laughed, and it made me feel *superior* to be the "life" of the party, to take the play away from others. But after awhile, I noticed that friends seemed to feel uneasy and uncomfortable in my company and that they began trying to avoid me. This commenced to worry and disturb me, and yet I was so dumb that I couldn't figure out the reason.

Finally, I decided to go to an older friend, to confide in him and ask him point-blank what was the matter with me—what I was doing that people didn't seem to like.

This friend studied me for a few minutes before speaking. Then he asked: "Are you sure you really want to know?"

"Yes," I answered. "I wouldn't have come to you if I didn't."

"Well," said my friend, choosing his words carefully. "This may hurt—but you've developed the habit of trying to be too smart. You seem to want to top what anyone else says, no matter what it is. You won't let others get any credit for their own remarks. You're like an actor who is always trying to steal scenes from everyone else on stage—and other people naturally don't like it. They resent your breaking in on them all the time, trying to be a big shot at their expense!"

This was a crusher, but I had asked for it. My friend had warned me that what he would tell me about myself would hurt. I can still feel the sting of his criticism. Why couldn't I have seen what I was doing to myself by these actions? Why couldn't I have realized that everyone likes a little attention, a little recognition, a little appreciation—and that no one likes someone who is thinking of himself, first, last and all the time?

This was a punishing experience to me, but I am glad it happened to me early in life. Since that time, when anything goes wrong, when I haven't been able to get along with others, or when I think I have been mistreated, I always get off by myself and take inventory, and try to "see myself as others may have seen me." Then I ask myself what I could have been doing, consciously or unconsciously, that helped bring some unhappy experience to me.

Invariably I have found that I have been either wholly or partially at fault. I am always relieved at this discovery, because I know I can start doing something about it. I can go to work, at once, correcting these attitudes and actions of mine that have been offending others. Doing it may hurt, but not half as much as it would if I were to wait until my faults became so big that everyone would know about them —and they would be doing me great personal harm.

Along this line, but of a somewhat different nature, another occasion taught me a bitter but valuable lesson. I feel I should tell it because an experience like this could just as readily happen to you, and probably has. None of us is perfect, quite obviously, and it is so easy for our ego to become inflated at times.

I had returned on a visit to the city of Marion, Indiana, where I had started my career as a writer, reporting for the *Marion Chronicle,* a daily. I was to be guest speaker at a banquet sponsored by the Junior Chamber of Commerce, of which I had formerly been a member. I had by then acquired a national reputation as a writer of boys' sport stories. Because I had written two novels based on the exploits of the Marion High School basketball team, I was being honored.

An hour or so before the banquet, several Marion friends took me bowling. Among them was Walker Farr, Marion's champion bowler. I had not bowled in a number of years and although I usually bowled better than average scores, I did not rate, in any way, with Farr. But this night, I suddenly got "hot." I let the ball out at just the right spot on the alley and reeled off strike after strike. Farr, at first, laughed at my luck, as did the others. Then, as I continued my streak and he began to fall behind in the score, the competition became serious. Incredibly, I finished with a score I still remember, one of the highest I had ever bowled—263!

Marion friends kidded Farr about this upset defeat he had suffered. Farr took it good naturedly and, in the best of spirits, we left the bowling alley for the banquet. If the matter had been dropped at that point, all would have been well.

Unfortunately, I had become a bit "heady" over my victory. When I was called upon to speak, I could not resist a little roast of Walker in my opening remarks. The moment I started, I realized I had made a mistake, that I couldn't pull the remark off in a way that would sound funny, without offending. But, once into the subject, I had to go through with it, a smile freezing on my face, while all those at the banquet stirred uncomfortably. I caught a glimpse of Walker Farr's face. It was red as fire.

I should have stopped and apologized then and there. But when you are caught in the middle of an embarrassing mistake, you usually try to get past it as quickly as you can, and that's what I did. I dropped what must have sounded like braggadocio comments and got into the main body of my talk, but it too went flat. Of course, it seemed far worse to me than kindly friends said it was. Now, after all these years—dredging this experience up from my subconscious and reliving it for whatever value it may be to you—I feel deep pangs of remorse.

How could I have done such a thing? How could I have been so ill-mannered, and before an audience of former hometown friends? How could I have let my ego run away with me? But it happened—and not because I hadn't known better. Which is proof that no matter how much knowledge we may acquire about our minds and emotions we must be on guard!

We are taught by life experience every day of our existence on this earth. That is, we are taught if we will learn and accept the lessons that experiences like those I have related can teach us.

No constructive purpose is served in putting up your defenses against wrong images that you find other people are holding in mind about you. Nor does it pay to resent or dislike them for it, or to pretend that you don't give a hang what they think about you.

In these times, a record is kept of almost every individual, either for credit or employment or social security purposes, if not criminal!

Questionnaires are often sent out to your friends and acquaintances, asking confidential information about you. What do they know about your character, your personality, your conduct, your reliability, your economic status, your religion, your club and fraternal affiliations, your community activities and so on?

These queries cause people to call to mind their over-all mental image of you, how you have impressed them in their contacts with you.

Ask yourself what most of them would say about you today.

If your own personal, hardboiled analysis tells you that

the image you are conveying to others is not what it should be, get busy on it. I hope and pray and believe that I am not going to repeat the mistakes I have made in the past. I may be tempted, under different pressing circumstances, to fall back into old habit patterns of thinking and acting, but I have suggested to myself that I will be made instantly aware of this relapse and that I will stop any repetitions or new mistakes before they start!

You can do the same!

One of the wisest men I have ever known, a man high in mental and spiritual development, said to me:

"Never for one moment forget this: *life is an individual proposition*. No matter how much you may wish, at times, to shift responsibility for your thoughts and acts to others, or to escape from the consequences of certain experiences in which you have become involved, you are living in a world of cause and effect—a world in which nothing actually happens by accident—and you, yourself, set up the causes by your own thinking, good or bad, for the things that happen to you!"

I have proved this time and again in my own life, and so have you, if you will only admit it to yourself. But when I've made this statement to some men and women, they've said to me: "That's a frightening thought. Do you mean that I have attracted failure, economic need, ill health, dislike, loss of friends, unhappiness. . . ." And when I have told such people, "Yes, if any of these conditions have come upon you, you have your own self to blame," they said, "But we didn't *picture* these things!"

No, perhaps they didn't, directly. They didn't *see* themselves failing, running short of funds, suffering a nervous breakdown, growing unpopular, losing friends, ending up unhappy. But their mental attitudes were expressed in this kind of thought:

"Wouldn't you just know this would happen to me?"

"There's no use trying—I just can't do it!"

"I don't want to meet him or her . . . I know I won't like them!"

"It's just my luck to have this happen. I'm always getting the worst of it."

"I don't care what So-and-So thinks of me. He'll have to take me the way I am!"

"Oh, I feel so bad, I wish I could die!"

"I'm going broke—there's no way out."

"Yes, I'm feeling fairly well today—but this doesn't mean anything. I'll probably feel worse tomorrow!"

Aren't these wonderful suggestions? Can you possibly picture, with the knowledge of mind you have now gained, how *any* of these thoughts could attract good?

On the contrary, this kind of thinking can only bring one result. Yet, many of us, carelessly, in moments of emotional depression, give voice to such thoughts and then wonder why so many things go wrong in our lives, why people don't have a better image of us and like us better.

PREPARE YOURSELF TO FACE ANYTHING!

So—take stock of yourself! We are living, as you know, in a terrific age—an amazing age. To many whose minds are unprepared, it is a bewildering, frightening age.

The tempo of life and developments is increasing at a rapid rate. Things are unfolding almost too fast for the mind of man to grasp. More and more earth-shaking developments are on the way. Much that was considered impossible a few years ago has already been accomplished. Anything may happen from now on—and probably will!

You must train yourself to be mentally alert, to maintain an open mind, to make contact with your creative power within, in order to adapt yourself to the changes that are coming, so that you will have the insight, the understanding and the courage to meet them and to deal happily and successfully with the people with whom you will be associated.

You must learn how to perceive the truth—to accept what appeals to your past experience, your reason and your intuition—and to reserve judgment on all things with which you are unfamiliar, until you can prove or test them in your own life.

It is not enough for you to learn the laws of mind. You must learn how to *use* your mind in accordance with these laws.

You've heard the old adage: "Faith without works is dead." You must *work* with yourself if you would develop the creative power within, so that it can do for you what it has done and is doing for others.

The fortunate men and women of the world are those who know how to visualize, how to eliminate their fears and worries, how to remain inwardly calm and poised no matter what the circumstances, how to assume a positive mental attitude and how to retain emotional stability under pressure.

This should be your great goal in life—to realize a like attainment. It will be your only guidance and protection in this fast-moving world of today.

ABANDON ALL LIMITED THINKING!

Prepare your mind now by putting aside all narrow and limited thinking. Never say again that *anything* is impossible, no matter how impossible it may seem at the moment. Don't restrict and shackle your mind by small and prejudiced thinking. Free your consciousness of feelings of resentment, antagonism, hate and like emotional reactions toward others. Such thoughts keep you from thinking straight, from getting the right perspective toward others and yourself. They are holding you back from progress, preventing your creative power from working through you.

You can overcome the effects that wrong thinking has had upon you. But to do this, you must gain emotional control; you must learn how to relax your physical body, how to make your conscious mind passive and how to place the right pictures of what you desire in mind. You must learn how to release the hold that past mistakes, now stored in your subconscious, have upon you.

Since "like attracts like" (I'm repeating this again!), good attracts good and bad attracts bad. It's as simple as that, but you can't straighten yourself out without facing your past.

Men and women say to me: "But I'm trying to *forget* my past!"

Alas, the mind doesn't operate that way. What it takes into consciousness, it hangs onto, unless you, through an act of recognition, resolution and will, *change* the picture or let go of it!

How often do you let yourself become upset about something someone does or says? You store the picture of each incident and feeling in your mind.

When you think of this person, you call up the same feelings against him, until you have overcome them. If you don't change them, they exist as irritations in consciousness. Irritations eventually find their reflection in some disturbed body condition or illness, or an unhappy human experience.

Do you want to permit these past irritations to attract similar disturbances in your future? Then get busy and eliminate them from your consciousness.

You know yourself better than any close friend or relative can ever know you. You may have been able to mask your real feelings and thoughts from others; but you can tell, deep down within, what you really think and feel about anything or anybody. If these thoughts and feelings are not good, get busy and *make* them good—because you can be certain others will sense these attitudes in time, if they haven't already!

Forgive others for what they've done to you. Assume your share of the blame. Don't hold resentments or grudges or hates. They are poisoning your mind and your body, upsetting the chemistry of your physical organism, making you susceptible to all possible types of diseases and illnesses. Doctors now attribute such afflictions as arthritis, asthma, rheumatism, shingles, some forms of epilepsy and many other sicknesses to nervous and emotional disturbances. It has even been found that many who have cancer can retard its progress if they can control their emotions and maintain an optimistic, fearless attitude toward it.

"That something" in mind has unlimited power to overcome, to heal, to create, to attract—once you learn how to use it.

The development of this power is up to you. Are you willing to put forth the effort? If you are, go with me, from chapter to chapter, studying and applying . . . studying and applying . . . and when we reach the end of this journey together, you will have the answer to your problems and will be on your successful, happy way—*alone*.

THOUGHTS TO BUILD INTO YOUR LIFE

In the interest of self-improvement, I will make every effort to see myself as others may see me.

When I discover that I have said or done something that has offended another or that has been misunderstood, I will go to that party or parties and apologize or do whatever is necessary to make amends and to correct any possible "wrong image" of me.

40

I will be constantly on guard against giving myself destructive suggestions which can attract bad or unhappy experiences to me.

I will refuse to hold hateful, resentful or disturbed pictures in my mind against others, knowing that they can only produce physical and mental irritations with a bad result ensuing.

I will forgive others for what they have done to me and accept my share of the blame or responsibility in the faith that good will eventually come out of the experience.

5

How to Remove Wrong Pictures from Your Mind

If you took your camera and went around shooting pictures of everything you saw or heard and every experience you were a part of, all day long, whether it was of any value to you or not, you would have the craziest hodgepodge of photographs imaginable, once developed.

You wouldn't know what to do with most of them except to throw them out—get rid of them as soon as possible so they wouldn't clutter up the place—regardless of how much they had cost you in time and effort and money.

Do you realize you are doing this to your mind all the time? You are exercising little or no selectivity in screening out the mental pictures your mind is constantly recording of all you see and hear and do, every waking moment!

You are taking in everything, the bad pictures with the good, storing them in your memory bank, along with the feelings you have had at the time.

If you have had a run-in with a neighbor, business associate, or member of the family and have had heated words, your impressions and feelings have been automatically registered. You can prove it to yourself by recalling them right this moment—mental pictures of the occurrence will instantly pop out of your memory storehouse and reenact themselves in your mind's eye. Not only that, but you will be conscious of the same feelings—just as when you see a sound film a second time.

This recording mechanism in your mind may be likened to a video tape that stretches back and back and back to the moment you were born, when you took in your first breath of air outside your mother's womb and uttered your first baby cry!

Yes, this has been demonstrated by hypnotists who have regressed subjects to the time of their birth—some of these people have been able to describe feelings relating to the moment of their arrival on this earth. Much that you are now unable to recall is stored in memory, not only your earliest babyhood but also many later events, so tragic or unpleasant that you have subconsciously walled them off and tried to forget or to avoid remembrance for all time.

These unresolved and unfaced experiences are holding you back in many areas of your life. To realize this, you must understand that your mind ordinarily functions by means of the association of one idea or subject to another.

For example, if you are away from home and you hear a cat meow or a dog bark, you may think of your own cat or dog, or recall some experiences you may have had with it, or even feel affection for it.

Someone tells you of an automobile accident he has had, and you, in sympathizing, immediately recollect a car accident of your own, which you relate.

This is all in accordance with the mental law I have been emphasizing: "Like attracting like" in the realm of mind!

YOU ARE WHAT YOU THINK AND FEEL!

Now, here is something you may not have considered: the sum total of all your present thoughts and feelings, remembered and unremembered, has made you what you are today!

The experiences that have had the deepest effect upon you have determined your mental and emotional attitude toward things. Let's take a simple illustration:

If, as a child, you were frightened by a dog that may have bitten you, you can call from memory the mental picture of what happened and you can even bring up the feeling you had at the time that the dog bit you. Of course, your memory, after all these years, will not be as vivid as it was shortly after you had the experience, but it is strong enough to prove to you that the mental picture and the feelings you had of the event are *still there!*

Now, if this experience set up a fear in you of dogs—unless you have done something to overcome this fear—you will still be afraid of dogs whenever they come near you or look as though they might bite.

Can you imagine now how many unhappy pictures of past experiences may be influencing your life today?

PROOF THAT YOU THINK IN PICTURES!

Despite the fact I have repeatedly stated that you think basically in mental pictures and not in words, I feel I should take "time out" to prove to you, once and for all, that this is so—that this operation of your mind is fundamental, that you can't get away from it, that you have to live with it and by it, and that your success and happiness absolutely depend upon what you PICTURE for yourself in life!

Now hear this:

Primitive man, before language was invented, had only one method of communication with his fellow man. He drew crude pictures on the walls of his caves, with charcoal, or chiseled images in stone. When he returned from the hunt, he would draw these pictures of his adventures so that members of his tribe could comprehend what had happened to him. Gradually, the same pictures began to stand for the same experience, and they took the form of symbols. They could then be abbreviated, and the merest suggestion of them would call to the mind of the observer, through association, the pictures or human experiences for which these symbols stood.

Eventually, symbols were combined to represent a whole chain of incidents, and finally became letters of the first alphabet, as man sought to find sounds to associate with them.

Thus language was born—and centuries later, the invention of the printing press made possible the wide dissemination of knowledge that has resulted in the so-called civilization we have today.

BUT, with all man's development—his acquisition of languages, his modern methods of communication—his MENTAL PROCESSES are still no different from those of his ancient ancestor, PRIMITIVE MAN!

You still *think* in MENTAL PICTURES, and you always will!

Example: If I ask you to tell me the outstanding thing that happened to you YESTERDAY, what do you have to do?

You must first, through an effort of WILL, call upon your MEMORY to produce for you MENTAL PICTURES of the experience you wish to relate.

Then as you SEE, in your mind's eye, this picture or pictures of yourself going through yesterday's experience, you put what you are seeing into WORDS and describe it to me.

But WORDS are just the sound symbols of what happened to you, so, as I listen, I must translate what you are saying back into MENTAL PICTURES in *my* mind—in order to SEE what experience you had.

Perhaps now you can better understand that in any exchange of thought you are dealing basically in the transmission of *mental pictures* from one mind to the other, at all times—through the medium of language.

You can think of NOTHING without first PICTUR-ING it in your mind!

We have spoken of the great creative power which exists as a part of your subconscious. This power is limited only by the *nature* of the thoughts or mental pictures you give it. It is through this marvelous creative power, as I have said, that man has been enabled to bring into the world all the ideas and inventions that have lifted him from the PRIMI-TIVE to the atomic age!

It cannot be reiterated too often: *What you picture in your mind, if it unites with the creative power within, can attract to you whatever you fear or desire.*

THE CREATIVE POWER IS LIKE A MAGNET

Give the creative power a strong, clear picture of what you want, and it starts to work magnetizing conditions about you—attracting to you the things, resources, opportunities, circumstances and even the people you need, to help bring to pass in your outer life what you have pictured!

You still have difficulty in believing it? Think back over your life! Recall the times you lived in fear that something would happen; eventually it came to pass. You perhaps didn't realize it, but those fear pictures had so impressed "that something" within, that you caused it to attract wrong conditions to you and made you susceptible to the very thing you feared.

You see, this creative power within doesn't reason. It just produces for you what you order in the form of a mental picture, with strong feelings of fear or desire behind it. That's why that inner power is TNT, either for or against you, depending on whether your thinking is constructive or destructive.

Now can you more clearly understand how certain good, as well as bad things have happened throughout your life? This creative power has been serving you constantly, and the kind of results you have obtained has depended upon the kind of mental pictures you have presented to it.

How does your life add up on this basis? Has it been filled, thus far, with about as many unhappy experiences as happy ones? If so, you'll want to change that in a hurry! And you can change it at once by a fundamental change in your mental attitude, by overcoming your fears and worries and replacing them with positive, confident courageous thinking.

There is no longer any doubt about it (and there never has been to those who have understood the operation of consciousness) that "as you *picture* in your mind and heart, so are you!"

Keep this great fact always before you. Let it dominate your everyday thinking. Check yourself each time you tend to become disturbed, mentally and emotionally, and to store unhappy, destructive mental pictures in your mind. Do you want to pass on such pictures for your creative power to work upon? Do you wish these fears or desires to be magnetized so that they attract similar experiences to you? If not, let go of this kind of picture at once. Change them for the better. Drop all feelings of fear or resentment or hate or jealousy, whatever these feelings may be, and substitute the right kind of feelings and mental attitudes. The moment you do so, you destroy the power these wrong pictures would eventually have over you.

REPLACING A BAD PICTURE WITH A GOOD ONE!

There is a technique for getting rid of bad mental pictures, of past fears and worries and hates and other destructive thoughts and feelings.

You have to have the courage to get off by yourself to review your past life, going back in memory to the times when these fears and worries and hates and like feelings originated. Unhappy, unpleasant or as tragic as these experiences may have been, if they have left deep scars in your mind that need erasing or releasing, you must face them once again, in your mind.

What you are preparing to do is to create a new mental picture, a new resolution in consciousness, based upon what you now realize you should have done or said, on how you should have reacted mentally and emotionally when faced with this original experience and others like it which you may have attracted throughout your life. If you cannot recall the first time you developed these fears and worries and hates, put your attention on the experiences of like nature that you DO recall.

You can depend upon it, if you have developed a fear or worry or hate in your past, it will still be with you unless you have removed it by assuming a new mental and emotional attitude concerning it!

Have you had the sensation of a tune suddenly coming into your mind and repeating itself again and again, despite every attempt you may make to get rid of it? This is an annoying and uncomfortable feeling, and it may have been brought about by your walking or doing something in a certain unconscious rhythm which fits the tempo of the song. "Like attracting like," the song bobs into consciousness from your memory storehouse and synchronizes with what you are doing and keeps on keeping on until you change what you are doing or thinking or feeling, then *zip* —the tune is gone! Gone back into your memory file, not to be experienced again until some other associative act or thought brings it to life!

Another effective way to eliminate a tune that has taken

possession of your consciousness is to think of another tune and start humming it to yourself, either aloud or in your mind. You can only be conscious of one thought at the same time, and this second tune, superimposed over the other, concentrated upon by you, causes the first tune to disappear. You lose your awareness or memory of it. In much the same way, a wrong or unwelcome thought or mental picture is removed from your mind by substituting a different thought or mental picture in its place.

PICTURE GOOD THINGS INSTEAD OF BAD

Once you have cleared your mind of wrong mental pictures and emotional reactions, you are ready to picture with faith and confidence the achievement of good things.

Faith is the *energizer* of the creative power, "that something" within. I'll have more to say about that later, but you must believe that what you picture can come to pass. Doubt will destroy your picture and demagnetize the creative power so that you will get a half-result or no result at all, or even a wrong result.

Picture whatever you desire as though it has already been achieved in mind. See yourself *having* something, *being* something or *doing* something, as if it were an accomplished fact. Don't try to picture the individual steps that you think you should take to get where you want to go. Your conscious mind is so limited in its operation—limited by your five physical senses—that it cannot know what is the best move for you to make or the best direction to take. But your subconscious mind, "that something" within, is not limited by time or space. It can function on all levels and in all directions at once, putting you in touch with all manner of opportunities and people that you do not even know of consciously as yet.

Whatever you need to fit into the pattern of achievement that you have pictured will be attracted to you by the power within if you persist in your visualizing of your heartfelt desire.

This is the simple technique to follow. It will produce infallible results in due course of time, if you master the art of *picturization*.

ARE YOU THE "VISUALIZING" OR THE "FEELING" TYPE?

But I should make clear that there are two types of minds—the *visualizing* and the *feeling!* If you find it difficult to create a clear picture in your mind's eye of what you want in life, don't strain in an attempt to do it. You are probably the *feeling* type ... and all you then have to do is to concentrate on an imaginary focal point in the dark room of your inner mind and let yourself *feel* that what you desire has been accomplished in consciousness, that all that remains is for it to be materialized by the magnetic creative power in your outer world. You will get the same result as those who find it easy to visualize.

THE SUGGESTIVE POWER OF PICTURES!

Because we think basically in *pictures,* we are influenced not only by the mental pictures that our minds record of whatever we think or do or feel but also by what we read and hear and see on radio and television.

Remember always: *What a man can picture in his mind he can, one day, do or attain in life!*

Let's apply this incontrovertible truth, for a moment, to the publishing and entertainment worlds!

What *kind* of pictures are being planted in the minds of readers of newspapers, magazines and novels; radio listeners, television viewers, theater-goers of stage and screen?

Thoughts are things; they are the world of tomorrow in creation—now!

Most human creatures are more swayed by their emotions than by their reasoning power. They are usually dominated by their *feelings*. Because of this, what they read, the radio programs they hear, the television shows they see, the stage and screen plays they take in, are having an immediate IMPACT upon their lives.

You are a member of the human family and you now have come to recognize the power of what your mind accepts in the form of mental pictures.

Ask yourself: "What effect is what I am seeing and hearing having upon me mentally and emotionally?"

Educators, spiritual leaders and law enforcement authorities are at last commencing to express concern over the preponderance of sex in advertising and various mediums of entertainment, the violence on TV, shoddy movies, pornography in books and magazines—and the devastating contribution these media are making to misconduct of young and old.

Those who desire to influence and control the thinking of great masses of people know the power of *picturization,* know how to arouse strong feelings for or against a situation or an issue, how to make individuals think what they want them to think—unless said individuals are awake and aware of this approach.

You do not have to accept the PICTURES that are being bombarded at you! If your mind is free of fears and worries and hates and prejudices and like destructive thoughts, it will recognize these wrong pictures whenever and wherever encountered, and you can reject them—refuse to let them become a part of your consciousness.

It cannot be stated too often: A *wrong* thought planted in your mind will always result in a *wrong* act in some future moment of time, unless counteracted by a *right* thought.

Each time you take in a wrong mental picture of a certain sexual desire, for example, it is reinforced by all the repressed sexual desires of like nature which already exist in your subconscious. Since, as I have reiterated, like attracts like, this creative power within, acting as your unquestioning, obedient servant, will one day find the opportunity for you to express your sexual craving in a physical act.

This is the way your creative power works, under any and all conditions, seeking to convert whatever you give it in the form of mental pictures, good or bad, into actual life happenings.

What kind of pictures do you have stored in mind? Are there some you would not wish to be reproduced in your outer world? Some you would not wish for even your close friends and relatives to know about?

There is great danger in wrong use of TNT, this power within you. Don't light the fuse with wrong mental pictures.

A little snowball, starting in the form of a minor fear or desire, starts rolling down a hill. It keeps on growing in size as it attracts more fears or desires of like nature. In the earlier stages of its expansion, it could be stopped by an act of will and a removal of the force of these accumulating fears and desires behind it. But now it is becoming so monstrous that it has a momentum of its own, and the individual who tries to check its downward path becomes engulfed in it.

What kind of a snowball are you rolling? The right or wrong kind?

You and you alone are responsible for what you think and how you feel about things. What you think and feel, multiplied by what everyone else on this planet thinks and feels, is going to determine not only your future, but theirs!

A change in their world and yours begins with *you!*

THOUGHTS TO BUILD INTO YOUR LIFE

I realize that whatever I have experienced in life, from the moment I was born, is now recorded in mental-picture-form along with the feelings I had at the time.

To keep from attracting more unhappy experiences of a certain nature, I must go back in memory, recall to mind and eliminate the original incidents which, like attracting like, are causing similar experiences in my present.

The elimination of these causes is accomplished by replacing these unhappy or fearsome memory images with positive mental pictures of what I should have said or done at the time.

In picturing what I hope to achieve in the future, I must visualize myself as already having accomplished what I desire to do or be or have —just as though I have photographed the completed objective.

I will be on the alert to protect myself against any negative thoughts or mental pictures others may be holding of me.

I will always remember that the image I maintain of myself is all-important to my happiness and success.

6

The Power of Relaxing Body and Mind

Can you relax at any time you wish? Let go of all tenseness that may be building up in your body and nerves? Let go of the fears and worries and excess feelings of responsibilities you may be carrying around mentally?

It is so easy in this high-pressure world to commence taking one's self too seriously, to try to do too much in too short a time.

Go down any busy street in any big or little town and study the people hurrying by on foot or in cars. How many of them look relaxed? How many of them actually look happy, contented?

Don't you see a "driven" expression in many faces?

Listen to the brakes scream as cars almost collide at a street intersection because no one wants to wait for the other fellow!

Meet someone you know. Does he or she ordinarily have time to stop and talk?

"Hello, where have you been? What you been doing? Where are you going? Oh, you don't have time to tell me! What have *I* been doing? Well, I don't have time to tell you, either. But let's get together when we have a few spare moments! You don't know what *year* that will be? Isn't it the truth? Just too busy to enjoy knowing each other!"

This could well be your conversation, slightly exaggerated, of course, but not too much. And what have you gained by saving a few minutes here and a few minutes there? Haven't you lost more in expenditure of mental and physical energy than has been good for you, health-wise? This all adds up day after day.

You gulp your meals and start belching with indigestion. Instead of slowing up, you reach for an aspirin or an anti-acid tablet, and at night you take sedatives and sleeping pills, possibly tranquilizers. You don't *naturally* relax, you just knock yourself out, then get up, often still groggy in the morning, and begin the rat race all over again.

Sooner or later, your system commences to rebel. It has taken so much punishment that it can't serve you efficiently any more. You get tight feelings in your head, painful, congested sensations in the nerve center in the back of the neck and in your stomach or solar plexus. You start wondering if you are propagating an ulcer or getting ready to have a stroke, and you even speculate that you may be headed for a nervous breakdown.

What to do? Double the aspirin tablets and assorted collection of "relaxatives" and "laxatives" and "extra energy suppliers"? Or, see a doctor or psychiatrist? You finally admit you've got to do *something*.

THE ANSWER CAN BE SIMPLE

Actually, in many instances, all you need to do is take yourself in hand, with the resolution to take time out each day for the specific purpose of relaxing your body and your mind.

Of course, this is the theory behind "coffee breaks" and "time-outs for tea," or a coke or a glass of milk! These are all "drinks in the right direction" but they don't get the basic job done. You may get a few moments' surcease from the "grind" but you are soon back at it again, and perhaps

55

it's a few nervous puffs on a cigarette, a pipe or a cigar, as an aid to release of tension. I know many men and women who keep a stream of barbiturates going into them, at different times during the day. They are not operating on normal body energies and cannot "let go" without outside stimulants or depressants.

I do not mean this to be an attack on the drug industry, but the more drugs you can ordinarily do without, the better off you will be.

Are you willing to invest five to ten minutes in midmorning, in midafternoon and at night to practice a simple method of relaxing body and mind which can so revitalize you that you will reduce your need for medication to the very minimum?

While you are deciding whether or not you can *afford* to make this investment, let me tell you of an experience I had with a top executive who couldn't make up his mind.

The indispensable man

Some time ago, in the Midwest, a friend took me to meet the general manager of a big automotive plant. He explained: "I'm afraid Mr. Trent is on the way to a nervous breakdown. His plant has been doubled in size in the past six months. He's been under increasing pressure—hardly eats or sleeps. I very much hope you can help him."

At nine o'clock the next morning, as we entered Mr. Trent's office and he arose to meet me, the telephone rang. It was a long-distance call from a branch plant in Toledo, Ohio. The moment he placed the receiver to his ear, his face turned livid.

"What?" he cried. "You haven't received that shipment? *Just a minute!*"

He pressed an intercommunication button and got a department foreman on the line.

"What in the blankety-blank is the matter?" he demanded. "Hasn't that shipment gone out yet?"

I could hear the foreman yelling back into the phone. This was a fine way to start the day. Mr. Trent had received an emotionalized charge from a disturbed executive in Toledo, had passed it through his body on down the line to his department foreman—and now *three* men were upset!

This matter was finally settled, and Mr. Trent hung up, only to have the phone ring again. Another trouble call— this time from Detroit. Once more, a highly aroused emotional atmosphere, another department head bawled out . . . and when this call was finished, a *third* trouble call—now Cleveland! More pushing of buttons, more disturbed emotions—all within a ten minute period!

At last Mr. Trent had a free moment, during which my friend introduced me to him.

"Glad to meet you, Sherman," said Mr. Trent. "What did you come to see me about?"

My friend broke in to explain that I was giving a series of lectures in the city, and that, as a feature of these lectures, I taught people how to *relax*.

"Relax!" said Mr. Trent. "That's for *me!*" He picked up the phone and said to his secretary. "No calls for ten minutes." Then, turning to me, he said: "Okay, I'm your man. Show *me* how to relax!"

I explained to Mr. Trent that I couldn't do it in so short a time, that his obviously tense condition had become chronic and that he would need to change his habits of a lifetime, his mental attitude. But if he wished to come to my lectures, I could promise him that in five evenings he would learn how to relax.

"Five *nights!*" exploded Mr. Trent. "Do you know what time I came here this morning? Seven o'clock. Do you know what time I left last night? Around one. Do you know when I have been seeing my wife and kids for the last six months?

Between six and seven each night, at dinner! . . . My super-intendent is in the hospital with a heart attack, three of my foremen are home sick—with nervous breakdowns and stomach ulcers. I admit—all my staff should take your lecture course, *but they just don't have the time!*"

I looked at Trent—a man close to forty who looked years older. He was a bundle of nerves, suffering from super tension, driving himself toward a physical, if not a mental, collapse.

"Mr. Trent," I said to him, "it's apparent to me *that you've got the time to KILL yourself, but NOT the time to SAVE your life!*"

He looked at me a moment, shocked, then shook his head grimly and replied: "I guess *that's just about the size of it.*"

From coast to coast, wherever I go, I have been meeting thousands of men like Trent—women, too—who are taking themselves too seriously, who have overestimated their importance, who have mesmerized themselves into thinking that the world can't get along without them. Yet, when they drop out because of overwork, sudden nervous breakdown, illness or accident, others are somehow found to carry on for them, maybe not as efficiently, but the world manages to go on—*without* them.

You can add years to your life by stopping right NOW and resolving that you are going to take time out each day to RELAX, to throw off the emotional disturbances and tensions that may be building up in you. If you are at work or at home, will you set aside the five to ten minutes I have suggested—ten, if possible—to get off by yourself each mid-morning and midafternoon?

Get away from the telephone . . . don't light a cigarette . . . don't take a drink . . . don't eat . . . stop everything . . . and just *let go*—let the God Power within take over for this period.

Ask yourself: "Am I going too fast? . . . Am I disturbed about anything? . . . Am I nervous and tense?"

If you are, release these wrong feelings. Let go of them. If you don't, they'll be building up in you all day and you'll carry them home with you at night. Worse than that, you'll take them to bed with you, and they're the most restless, murderous bedfellows on earth.

The longer you keep these feelings inside you the more they'll pull you apart. Make this an *absolute* rule. Never, never EAT while you are emotionally upset! While you are under pressure, with disturbed thoughts running through your mind, your stomach tied up in knots, a tight feeling in the nerve center in the back of your neck and in your solar plexus—DON'T eat when you feel like this! Take as long as is necessary to throw these feelings off, to let go, to relax. If you force food into your body when it is not ready to receive it, you are *killing* yourself by degrees.

If you desire to improve the state of your health, you must make yourself receptive to the healing power of the TNT within you, but you can't go on breaking the LAWS of health and expect a permanent healing of physical ills and battered nerves.

YOUR FORMULA FOR GOOD HEALTH!

This is the simple method or procedure that thousands of men and women have used to relax body and mind and to picture not only good health but the things in life they have most desired. With practice, and "following through" with these mental and physical directives, you can take complete control of your body and your mind. Try it this very instant! Say to yourself and mean it:

I now relax my body . . .

I make my feet and legs comfortable . . .

I rest my hands and arms in my lap . . .

I let the chair hold my entire weight . . .

I let go of the body with my mind . . .

I leave all fears and worries behind . . .

I feel lighter—all physical tenseness is gone . . .

I close my eyes and shut out the world around me . . .

I turn the attention of my thoughts inward and become un-self-conscious of my body . . .

I now feel that I am existing only in consciousness . . .

A feeling of great inner peace and quiet begins to come over me . . .

In this moment of quiet—this inner stillness—I describe in words and also present in mental picture form, what I feelingly desire . . .

If it is better health, I picture healing energy permeating every cell and organ of my body, renewing and revitalizing it . . .

If I seek new opportunities and achievements, whatever they may be, I picture myself already having received them . . .

Then, through an exercise of faith, I set up in myself a confident expectation that what I have visualized will come to pass in my outer life . . .

That all the resources and developments I need are on their way to me in time . . .

And that I will be led by my creative power and my intuition to be at the right place at the right time— protected and guided every day throughout my life.

Herein, adapted to your needs and desires, is a priceless technique for controlling and directing your Subconscious —the creative power of TNT within you. You gain this control by relaxation of body and mind. These are the fundamental steps that must be taken. They should be practiced every day. By repetition you will get so that you can sit down and go through the process of letting go, mentally and physically, almost instantly.

For example, I can be actively engaged in mind and body, as I am in this moment of dictating these words, and yet, did I so choose, I could leave my desk, stretch out on the divan in my study, relax and be asleep within less than a minute! I do this a number of times each day, when I become aware that I am tiring and getting tensed up. When I lie down and "let go," I give myself the suggestion that I will sleep for from five to fifteen minutes, as I desire, and will awaken at the end of that time, refreshed in mind and body—and this *happens!* If this seems unusual to you, you must remember that I have had years of practice at this technique. But it does not take *you* years to learn it. You can acquire this same ability in a short time.

EACH INDIVIDUAL HAS A DIFFERENT RHYTHM OF THOUGHT AND EXPRESSION

Each of us, however, does not acquire knowledge or get onto "the hang of things" as speedily as others. Not realizing this, many of us consider ourselves dumb or incapable when we are not.

Science is just discovering that each person has a rhythm, a tempo of movement and thought that is natural to him, and which he should determine for himself and learn to stay within.

When you try to speed up your "natural tempo" beyond its normal functioning and physical and mental limitations, you lose your efficiency of thought and action.

"I can't think or make the right decisions when I'm hurried," many men and women say.

"I've learned never to make up my mind on an important matter right away," others have said. "I usually sleep overnight on it."

Still others may declare: "I operate on snap judgment. I am able to make right decisions quickly. If I mull things over too long, I seem to get muddled and lose my sense of judgment."

All these people are unconsciously revealing the different "tempos" of their individual beings.

"I can't match wits with people," someone may say, indicating not that he is less smart, but that his mind operates on a different tempo. He is out of synchronization with the person whose mind and tongue operate in a faster rhythm.

It is well to recognize this difference in temperament, personality and "mental and physical vibration." Getting tense and worried about it, and comparing yourself unfavorably to other people, can upset your health. But discovering your own natural speed of thought and action can help you overcome feelings of insecurity and inferiority.

It may not be true at all that you are less capable and bright than others. Given an opportunity to express yourself "in your own timing," you may reveal just as great, if not greater, intelligence than the faster operating friend or associate whose mental faculties are geared to speedier responses.

You can train your mind to react more quickly to experiences, but this simply means developing a keener alertness to your own tempo.

NO TWO PEOPLE EXACTLY THE SAME

Years ago, when I entered the Ford Motor Company at Highland Park, Michigan, as an unskilled laborer and was put to work on a machine turning out triple gears, I learned the secret of "tempo."

I saw men from all walks of life, some mechanically inclined and some not, trained to perform the operations of these machines. No two caught on to the operation with equal speed. Some mastered the operation within an hour or two. Others required several days. Past experience in mechanics helped, of course—but once a man became familiar with the machine and how it functioned, his speed of production depended upon his own "mental and physical rhythm."

Some just could never be "driven" to equal the production of others. Speeding the machine in an effort to compel the men to perform their physical actions faster only slowed them and even damaged the gears which were being manufactured. Left to their "own tempo," once their individual, natural speeds of movement of mind and body were determined, the men turned out satisfactory quantities of gears per hour.

If the reactions of some of these workers were too slow, they were transferred to other departments and jobs where they were fitted to serve in a useful and profitable capacity.

Thank heaven we DO all have *different speeds* of thinking and operation, because the various important tasks of the world require all this diversity of tempos for their successful completion.

If you have not discovered your own tempo, take time out to determine it. When you have, stop trying to work against it. Find employment suited to this tempo, and you will achieve far greater success in life and be infinitely happier! This applies as well to the friends and loved ones with whom you are associated. Adapt yourself to their rhythms of thought and action, as you would wish them to adapt to yours . . . and the tensions between you should be greatly relieved.

"I get along well with animals," a wise man once said to

me, "because I never try to make a dog meow like a cat, or a cat bark like a dog!"

Relax. Don't take life or what others think and do too seriously. You have enough to do to keep yourself on an even keel. Hit your stride and maintain it without pushing or forcing. There will be another day, so don't try to live up your tomorrows before they arrive. And remember to set aside times each day to give your body and your mind the "pause that refreshes." In this high-pressure world, you can't keep going indefinitely without it. Get over any fixed idea that you are a super man or woman. Without health, whatever hopes you have for reaching your goals in life are greatly diminished, if not obliterated. If you get nothing else out of this book but the ability to relax, to free your mind and body of daily tensions, no amount of money will pay for its value to *you*.

THOUGHTS TO BUILD INTO YOUR LIFE

The ability to relax body and mind, at will, is absolutely essential to my health and general welfare.

As a means of removing all tensions, I will invest five to ten minutes, morning and afternoon, more if necessary, and devote this time toward "letting go"—physically and mentally.

During these periods of relaxation—I will get away from the telephone; I will not smoke or take a drink or eat. I will stop everything—as I ask myself: "Am I going too fast? . . . Am I disturbed about anything? . . . Am I nervous and tense?"

Having done this, I will release these wrong feelings which are building up in me so that they do not become chronic.

Above all, I will refuse to eat, at any time, when I am under pressure or emotionally upset, knowing that this practice, in time, can be ruinous to my health.

Lastly, I will not permit myself to take life, or what others may think about me, too seriously.

7

The Magnetizing
Power of Decision

Do you have the *power of decision?* Can you decide what you want? No good and worthwhile thing can ever be achieved if you are unsettled and uncertain in your mind. Those who can't decide, who can't make up their minds, are always in trouble of one kind or another.

Ever play with a magnet and iron filings? Point the magnet in one direction and all the iron filings will regroup themselves along the line of force that has them in its grip. Turn the magnet away from this area, and the iron filings scatter into new formations. Move the magnet first one way and another, and the iron filings seem not to know where they're going.

They're like the woman driver who crashed into a bus at the corner of 42nd Street and Fifth Avenue in New York City. The traffic cop rushed up to her and demanded: "What happened? Why didn't you signal?"

"I *did* signal!" insisted the woman, indignantly.

"You *did?*" said the bus driver. "*I* didn't see it!"

"Then you must be blind!" said the woman. "I clearly signaled that I wasn't certain *which* way I wanted to turn!"

Do you know which way in life you want to turn? Do you know yourself well enough—your desires, your abilities, your temperament, your needs—to judge what is *best* to do as problems arise? Or like this woman driver, are you inclined to turn in TWO directions at the same time?

The world is divided into two classes of people: the "I Will-ers" and the "Should-I-or-Shouldn't-I-ers?" The latter class includes the great majority of men and women.

How many times have you said to yourself: "Should I or shouldn't I?" More human lives have been wrecked on the shoals of indecision than from any other cause.

"That something," the creative power within, cannot magnetically attract things to you unless it is magnetized by your decision. And you have to point this magnetic power of your mind in the direction you intend to go. When you do, it instantly commences to attract all the elements you need to help you get what you want.

When you are pulling against yourself mentally and emotionally, you are temporarily confusing, stalemating and even destroying your magnetic powers of attraction. An unsettled condition of mind and body can only attract unsettled conditions. It has no power to attract anything else.

The great lament of thousands upon thousands of human beings is: "I can't make up my mind!" This is one of the saddest dirges ever to rise from human hearts because it sounds the death knell of hope, ambition, self-confidence, initiative, accomplishment.

As long as you can't make up your mind, you are comparatively helpless, unable to move in any direction with assurance or with any feeling of safety and security.

"My mind is like an unmade bed," one woman said to me. "It's all in a jumble. I'm afraid to make it up. I'm afraid to touch it for fear I'll make it even worse. I guess I'll just leave it as it is!"

Do you wish to remain where you are now? If you do, just don't make up your mind! Unless you change your thinking, you will stay in whatever position you find yourself. Or you will sink to a lower position, because nothing stands still in life. It moves either up or down. Metal rusts if nothing is done to keep it polished and free of disintegrating forces.

You can't drop behind in the parade of life. You must keep going, for your own sake, at any age. Nature abhors anything that surrenders its usefulness. The buzzards are always waiting to do a cleanup job on forms of life that give up the struggle. Sounds pretty grim? It's not meant to be. Something has been provided to take care of everything, in all the various stages of life activity and in what is called death. In your body, millions of old cells are dying and new cells are being born, all the time. You are unconscious of it.

The same is true of ideas. As you grow in experience, you are killing off old ideas in your mind and giving birth to new ones. If you don't do this, the old, outmoded ideas clog up your mind, slow up your thinking, rust your brain, retard your progress and eventually bog you down.

If you are finding that you can't make decisions the way you used to, it's probably because you are wrestling with old ideas, old thought patterns, old habits and desires that you can't relinquish even when your "voice within" tells you to throw them overboard, get out of the rut and begin to do what you inwardly know you *should* be doing.

> Have you come to the Red Sea place in your life,
> Where, in spite of all you can do,
> There is no way out, there is no way back,
> There is no other way but through?
>
> Annie Johnson Flint

If this is your state of mind and situation in life at the moment, it is good! If your back is against the wall, if you've been pushed by indecision and circumstances of your own conscious or unconscious creation, as far as you can go, there is "no other way but through."

So face reality. Reorient yourself, reorganize your

scattered forces, *make up your mind,* and move straight ahead!

DECIDE—THEN ACT!

Many men and women have reached the seeming limit of their endurance only to find new strength awaiting them in their hours of desperate need, once they made a positive decision—once they said to themselves and meant it, "I'll face it. I'll see this thing through!"

There is no eleventh hour too late wherein "that something," the creative power within, cannot be magnetized by right thought and right decision and give you the strength and wisdom to pull out.

"God spoke to me in my great moment of need," thousands of grateful men and women have testified. They mean that they finally were driven to call upon their God-given inner resources after trying everything else and failing . . . and the inner power that they might have used all along answered their summons!

STOP BEMOANING YOUR FATE— GET WISE TO YOURSELF!

You have only two choices. You can go either higher or lower. You may take to drink or help yourself to a first-class nervous breakdown or wander around through the rest of your life, moaning about "what might have been" if you had only lived your life differently—while telling yourself, "It's too late now."

But if you belong to that smaller percentage of men and women who have "gotten wise to themselves," you discover that it is never too late to get on the right track. It is human to make mistakes, human to permit certain emotional desires to get the better of us, to carry us far afield from our real purposes and potentialities in life.

"I knew better but I did it, anyway," many sadder and wiser people say after they have gotten a new hold on themselves and snapped out of their departure from sane, happy, healthful living.

If you have reached the snap-back stage, *now* is the time. There is no other time for you but *now*. If you don't do it *now*, you'll never do it. You have reached your *moment of decision!*

"*There is no way out, there is no way back, there is no other way but through!*"

Take the plunge! Pull yourself out! Face whatever you have to face and get it over with. The longer you delay, the harder it will be.

Take direction from your real self within, follow its urgings no matter how difficult that may seem at the moment, ask forgiveness of those you have wronged, clear up all past resentments and hatreds, free your consciousness of past fears and inhibitions, so that your mind can become a channel for good thoughts and can begin to help you attract good things!

Get away forever from David Harum's indecisive: "Yes, an' no, an' mebbe, an' mebbe not!"

This will never get you anywhere. Who wants to live a miserable "Yes an' no" and "mebbe an' mebbe not" existence?

"I'd rather make a wrong decision and do something about it than make no decision at all," a successful business man said to me. "If I'm on my toes, I can usually tell whether a decision is wrong or not, before it hurts me too much—and out of this wrong decision, I then have the wisdom to make the right one. But if I make no decision at all, I get nowhere."

If indecision has you in its grip, *break* this lifetime habit. If you don't, you'll be miserable the rest of your life and your percentage of wrong decisions will attract many more wrong conditions to you.

A LIFE RUINED BY INDECISION

My grandfather's life was ruined by indecision. He had been a minister, but the more he studied the Bible, the more he was assailed by doubts. He felt it was blasphemous to question anything in the Bible, but he found himself increasingly unable to accept certain concepts.

He began to ask himself: "Should I keep on preaching— the way I now feel—or shouldn't I? Is it honest for me to continue to present some things that I no longer believe? . . . Should I confess my doubts to my wife, who is a devout believer? . . . What will my friends and loved ones think— the members of my congregation? . . . Will I be condemned for thinking as I do?"

This turmoil of indecision in his mind began to affect his health. He dreaded the approach of Sundays, when he would have to occupy the pulpit and, without faith and conviction, preach sermons. Oh, if only something would happen to give him a legitimate excuse to avoid preaching! And something *did!* He caused the power of TNT to serve him in a *negative* way. It gave him the excuse he was seeking!

My grandfather suddenly developed severe attacks of asthma just before church services. He became so short of breath that others had to substitute for him! These attacks steadily worsened and he was finally eased out of the ministry.

Everyone sympathized with him; no one condemned him, except himself. And for *thirty years* after that, my grandfather sat on the sidelines unable to make up his mind, unable to decide a new course of action, fearful of confessing his doubts to anyone, living a life of inner torment, suffering violent attacks of asthma every time he tried to wrestle with his problem!

Never will I forget, when, as a young man, I stood at the bedside of my grandfather as he was dying.

He said to me: "Oh, Harold—*if I only had my life to live over!* I would have expressed my convictions honestly and openly, because I realize now, too late, that many men and women were thinking as I was thinking—that it wasn't wrong to think that way, that I might even have expressed my thoughts in my own church. But I let fear and indecision and self-condemnation *keep me from my real lifework!*"

Let's hope that *you* are not plagued with indecision to this extent. This experience of my grandfather had a profound effect upon me. I resolved then that I would develop the power of decision. I would gain sufficient understanding of myself and sufficient control of my emotions to know what I *really* wanted, to *make up my mind* about it and to stick to it!

Of course, I have made wrong decisions. We all have, and we all will. But, increasingly, as I have learned to listen to the "Voice within," to follow the guidance of my intuition, I have been able to reduce the number of wrong decisions. You, too, will be able to do this.

Decision is born of courage, and courage springs from faith in self and in the God Power within. Why go on picturing a continuation of the problems and conditions that may be surrounding you now?

Decide to do away with them by resolutely changing the pictures, thus giving "that something" within the power to change your future for the *better!*

THOUGHTS TO BUILD INTO YOUR LIFE

I realize that, to achieve anything worthwhile
in life, I must have the power of decision. . . .

That lack of decision is unsettling and paralyzing, and that people who cannot make up their minds are always fearful and uncertain and unable to cope with life. . . .

That, whether any decision I may make is proved right or wrong, I am at least moving in some direction, and I am in a position to change my course of action as needed . . .

That the moment I decide what I should do, I magnetize conditions around me and start attracting the circumstances and people I need to meet whatever situation I may be facing . . .

That decision inspires self-confidence and courage, and frees my mind for positive action!

8

The Power of Overcoming Fears and Worries

Who or what would you say is your *Number One Enemy in Life?*

Some individual who has done you "dirt," taken advantage of you financially, stolen the affection of a loved one, injured your health, dominated your life, held you in personal or economic bondage, betrayed your confidence, forced you to do things you haven't wanted to do or given you a bad name by saying slanderous things about you?

All pretty bad—pretty unpleasant occurrences! Certainly anyone who would do these things to you could be characterized as an *enemy!* But you have a far worse enemy than any one or more persons, who can do you harm.

That enemy is . . . FEAR!

No human creature ever born has not known the sensation of *fear.* With many of us, fear has become almost second nature. In the young, fear serves a useful purpose since it develops caution. But the mature mind of the adult was not meant to be ruled by fear. And yet, conscious or unconscious fears are affecting most of us in one way or another!

The majority of your fears are carry-overs from childhood. Fear of the dark, fear of falling, fear of fire, fear of pain, fear of meeting people and so on are often memories of early past experiences.

If you have found yourself seeking to avoid facing a situation as you know you should, it is not because you are basically more cowardly than another. It is simply because you have less control over your emotions. Under the influence of fear, you have pictured yourself being hurt, physically or mentally, and your subconscious mind, acting upon this picture, has caused the thing feared to happen. And you *fear* it happening *again!*

"I know I'm weak but I just can't face it," you've heard people say. Such individuals have usually magnified certain conditions in their own minds until the mere thought of a situation has been enough to down them.

If you are in the midst of a group of persons and something unexpected and possibly tragic in nature happens, some of the group will instinctively stand up to it; others will seek to run away; still others will be caught in a state of mental and physical paralysis, unable to think or act. These different reactions to the same happening illustrate that each member of the group has developed greater or lesser control over his or her emotions.

Fear indicates a lack of balance between your outer and inner Self. The proper adjustment toward an external experience has not been made by the "real you," otherwise, your fear of this happening would have ceased to exist.

You fear only that which you have not conquered in yourself. Each time another experience of which you are afraid happens, and you permit your old fear of it to react upon you, you are only making that fear stronger and making yourself less and less able to meet similar situations as they occur.

No two people have had quite the same emotional reactions to past experiences. That is why some of us are strong where others are weak and weak where others are strong. Certain fears that you have conquered may still plague those near and dear to you. And something that would not concern them in the slightest, may bring terror to you. *It is a matter of record that General Anthony Wayne, fearless in battle, was deathly afraid of a bat.*

YOU MUST CONSTANTLY CONTEND AGAINST FEAR

Each day of your life you are, as you know, being called upon continually to face a series of situations. Perhaps one day it's sickness in the family, and your mind immediately pictures the worst. Perhaps you have been out of work for weeks or months and you have grown despondent, seeing nothing ahead but extended unemployment, the loss of your home—yes, you may even picture the loss of everything you consider worthwhile. Perhaps you are in love and are afraid you cannot win the object of your affections. Perhaps you almost drowned at one time in your life and have been left with a terrifying fear of the water.

There are hundreds of such situations to be faced and just as many emotional reactions to them as there are people, each reaction forming a vivid mental picture that is photographed upon your subconscious mind and becomes not only a part of your memory but a part of your emotional nature.

If an experience has developed fear within you, this same fear will be called forth when another similar experience arises. And each time you let this fear take possession of you, you increase the hold that the thing feared has upon you. Not only that, but you intensify the mental picture which this fear compels and make just that much more certain that your subconscious mind will bring this unpleasant picture to pass in your external life!

76

FEARS AFFECT YOUR HEALTH

Unrealized by you, your fears are constantly exerting an effect upon your nervous system and disturbing the health of your body!

The average human body is a "fire trap" of uncontrolled emotions. You possess a "highly inflammable" nerve network which, when touched off by one "spark" in the form of a *fear reaction,* can "fire" the consciousness on an instant's notice. This "emotional conflagration" throws up such a "smoke screen" about one's consciousness—so befuddles an individual's mind—that he is choked and confused, unable to find any *logical* exit from the existing emergency.

Paralyzed by fear, with your nervous system temporarily "burned out," you are like the trunk lines of a telephone system, which, when short-circuited, can carry no proper impulses. Under such circumstances, your mind finds it difficult, if not impossible, to reestablish connection with throbbing nerve centers and thus regain control of the body.

When you consider the many times you may have experienced the sensation of fear as you have encountered certain happenings in life, you can begin to understand the multiplied force you are mathematically building up within yourself—a destructive emotional charge that produces toxic poisons in your body, contributes toward the breakdown of your nervous system and harmfully reacts upon vital organs.

You cannot afford physically, mentally, emotionally and spiritually to be ruled any longer by fear!

Life's experiences are intended to make you ultimately face yourself—face *reality*. But your tendency is to put off unpleasant admissions of weakness in yourself as long as possible. This is human nature. But the longer you postpone meeting the situation, the more difficult it becomes to free yourself of your fears and the greater penalty you pay for letting them dominate you.

Everyday fears are, of course, those that concern you most —little agitating fears which, when added all together, amount to a series of destructive emotional reactions.

In my first book of a philosophic nature, *Your Key to Happiness*, I listed a number of common fears and asked readers to identify those with which they were afflicted. One woman wrote me a despairing note. She said: "Good heavens, Mr. Sherman—I've got them *all!*"

Well, here is that same list of fears! Take a rundown of them and ask yourself how many of them are at present victimizing *you?* If very few of these fears have a hold upon you, you may congratulate yourself on being far above the average human in nerve control. Here they are:

> Fear of being in high places
> Fear of falling
> Fear of water
> Fear of certain animals
> Fear of thunder and lightning
> Fear of fire
> Fear of crowds
> Fear of disease
> Fear of infection
> Fear of pain
> Fear of old age
> Fear of meeting people
> Fear of what others may think
> Fear of being alone
> Fear of poverty
> Fear of the "worst always happening"
> Fear of being locked in a room
> Fear of what may befall loved ones
> Fear of death

These are just a few of the fears that daily assail many of us. How many did you feel were yours? How many have you overcome? If some of these fears are today *ruling* you, it is because you consciously or unconsciously recognize an inability within yourself to meet a given situation. You have learned to control your emotions in some circumstances but not in others.

Take a moment to sit quietly before you read further, while you review this list of fears and try to recall how those that have affected you first got their hold upon you. Then return to this point and let me present to you a technique of thinking that will help free you from any or all of these fears.

Well, are you ready to go on from here? If you have really relived some past experiences during which you were gripped by fear, you have remembered that the chemistry of your body was upset. You have had heart palpitation, indigestion, shortness of breath, nervous perspiration, severe nervous tension, allergic reactions and a host of other physical disturbances while obsessed by fear.

You've heard the old saying: "You don't get ulcers from what you eat—you get them from what's eating *you!*"

President Franklin Delano Roosevelt made one terrific statement when he said: *"The only thing we have to fear is fear itself!*

He knew whereof he spoke. Millions of people who heard him make this declaration knew that he knew, because they had only to check the effect of fear in their own lives to realize that fear itself was even worse than the things feared!

It is often easier to face something you have feared than it is to anticipate the facing of it, because your imagination usually exaggerates, through fear, what you are afraid may happen to you. Many people are ashamed when they finally meet a situation they have feared, only to find it isn't nearly as bad or difficult as they had thought it would be.

ELIMINATE YOUR FEAR PICTURES

You should always remember, and this fact must be pounded home, every wrong picture which, with intense feelings of fear behind it, enters your consciousness, is like a seed that takes root in mind and eventually reproduces similar happenings in your life.

To protect yourself from the increasing effect of wrong emotional reactions, or your occurring and recurring fears, you must acquire the ability to control your feelings. You are still, more or less, a victim of fear and worry if you catch yourself expressing your feelings and apprehensions like this:

> "I'm so worried, I can't think straight."
> "I'm afraid to take a chance."
> "I've a feeling that nothing I try to do will turn out right."
> "I've lost faith in myself—and in God."
> "I can't get over what happened to me."
> "I know better, but I can't help burning with hate and resentment and fear."
> "I've lost all interest in living—I'd put myself out of the way if I weren't afraid to do it.
> "The doctor says if I don't learn to control my fears and worries, I'll kill myself."

Does this sound like you or like remarks you have made? If it does, it's time you were getting busy and eliminating this negative, defeatist attitude.

Fear always attracts wrong conditions; courage repels these same conditions and attracts the right ones in their place.

The first step to be taken in the removal of fear from your consciousness is to face squarely up to it. Take one fear at a time. See this fear exactly as it is and how ridiculous it has been for you to have permitted this fear any power over you. As you examine this fear, your conscious mind may try to tell you that it is silly to hide under the bed or in a closet during an electrical storm. But when you actually see lightning and hear thunder, your fear emotion takes over, destroys your reasoning and makes your hiding away seem, for the time being, a sensible thing to do. Anything may appear sane and right when your emotions are in control—and nothing can be more dangerous or damaging to you than these same emotions while they are dominating mind and body.

When under the influence of fear it is rarely possible to bring your emotions under control, because your emotional reaction will be too strong. But this control can be developed *now,* while you are relaxed and mentally at ease, able to analyze your past actions and let your reason tell you how useless and groundless most of your fears are.

Look back upon the most outstanding fear-ridden moments of your life. Relive these incidents on what I call the "motion picture screen" of your inner mind. As you recall these happenings, you will feel again, as you probably did when you checked the list of fears, the sensation of fear which each happening aroused.

Reviewing this experience in your mind's eye, you can see clearly, through exercise of your reason, what your right attitude *should* have been—how you *should* and *would* have met the situation had fear not kept you from it.

Now, hold the picture of this unhappy scene in your mind, and while you are holding it there, superimpose another picture—of what you now realize you should have said and done at the time. Mentally see yourself overcoming this fear. See yourself meeting any similar situations that may arise in your present or future, with your emotions under control, with courage and confidence in your ability to face whatever is to come.

ERASE ALL FEAR PICTURES AS THEY COME UP

Every time you feel the inclination to fear, stop the mental picture which the fear emotion forces upon you and take conscious command of yourself. Tell your inner or subconscious mind that it is to pay no heed to fear pictures, that will immediately erase each fear picture from consciousness by visualizing a picture of yourself fearlessly meeting the situation. By *repeatedly* seeing yourself having the proper emotional reaction to whatever happens, you will continue to lessen the hold that certain fears have upon you until, in due course, these fears will vanish completely.

Aviators, perhaps without knowing the law of the subconscious mind, nevertheless realize that they must overcome a wrong mental picture or have disastrous results. Whenever a student pilot has cracked up in a plane, if he has not been injured, he is commanded by his superior officer to get into another ship immediately and take to the air again in order to erase the memory of his "crash" landing.

Those who fear disease and infection should consider the religious bathers in the Ganges River, few of whom ever contract any sickness from its germ-infested, death-polluted waters. Here is a case where an almost sublime faith, coupled with an emotional frenzy, develops against surrounding contamination a resistance that has been the wonder of the medical world. Stark evidence that mind can and does play an important part in the operation and control of our external life!

Fear of being in high places has often been induced by a subconsciously recorded fall that may have occurred in infancy, with a resultant instinctively negative reaction to heights. Fear of height is frequently associated with fear of falling, and discovering the source of your one fear emotion will remove both.

If you have been disturbed by height, the next time you are in a high building or at a lofty elevation consciously visualize the firm, safe position of your body, thus supplanting the picture of your body hurtling through space. Only one mental impression can be entertained by your consciousness at any one moment, and this visualization will do away with your fear picture. If you look straight down from your height, do not mentally take your body to the street or ground. Let your eye alone cover the distance, while you remain *consciously aware* that your body is securely rooted in your present position. A little practice of this mental attitude will free you from fear of heights and falling.

REASON HELPS DESTROY FEAR

When you have convinced yourself inwardly that your fears are, for the most part, foolish and serve no constructive purpose, you will have dealt them a mental blow from which they cannot recover. It is *you* who have been keeping your fears alive, and *you* who must kill them off if you would not have them, in time, destroy you.

You can train your conscious mind so that it will challenge each fear emotion the instant you sense any fear. You can build courageous thought pictures to wall out your fears entirely. And you can take such command of yourself when facing a hazardous situation that, instead of giving way to your fear emotions, you can consciously see yourself being carried safely through your experience. Your subconscious mind will do the rest, causing you intuitively to make the right move at the right moment.

Worry, of course, is the handmaiden of fear. George Washington Lyon has said: *"Worry is the interest paid by those who borrow trouble."*

John Bunyan said he was able to eliminate worry from two days of each week. He wrote:

> There are two days in the week about which and upon which I never worry. Two carefree days, kept sacredly free from fear and apprehension. One of these days is yesterday . . . And the other is tomorrow!

Now, if you can eliminate fear and worry from yesterday and tomorrow, you have only to eliminate it from *today*, and you have it licked!

Ah! But today, as I have tried to emphasize, is the only time you are alive. Today is the only time you have to face reality. Today is the only time you have to *do* anything constructive or destructive. Today, before it becomes *yesterday* is your opportunity to go forward or backward! Today, before it becomes *tomorrow* is your chance to lay a better foundation for your future!

What are you doing with today? Are you filling it full of your usual fears and worries, thus guaranteeing that tomorrow will be a repetition of today?

HOW FAMED ARCTIC EXPLORER CONQUERED FEAR!

On the eve of Sir Hubert Wilkins' ill-fated submarine expedition under the polar ice, I spent some time with him. I was curious to know how this famed explorer felt about the hazards he knew he would have to face, what his actual feelings and thoughts were at the time of facing them. When opportunity afforded, I asked him, "Do you experience fear when you are face-to-face with a great emergency, perhaps death?"

I shall never forget the quiet expression of amusement with which Sir Hubert greeted my query.

> "I have never known the sensation of fear when I have been undergoing a dangerous or perilous experience," he

answered. "That is because *before* leaving on an expedition I have fought and overcome my fears of everything possible that might happen. I have looked ahead and tried to anticipate mentally everything that might go wrong. One fears only that which he cannot understand or for which he feels himself to be unprepared. I make it my duty to prepare for every conceivable emergency. I try to foresee the bad breaks which might be physically impossible to prevent, and to work out a plan for overcoming and surviving these breaks when and if they happen.

As a result, when I am on my expedition and suddenly find myself in a tight place, my mind immediately leaps to the solution of the problem—taking complete mental and physical command so that any fear emotions don't have a chance. In other words, I have visualized myself meeting any and all situations successfully, and fear, as a consequence, has no hold upon my consciousness. It simply *does not* and *cannot* exist!"

I have met few men of the character and calibre of Sir Hubert Wilkins. He understood thoroughly and utilized to a profound degree, the great creative powers of his subconscious mind. He once told me that he had mentally seen himself doing everything that he later accomplished; he also stated, following our extended experiments in long-distance telepathy over distances of two to three thousand miles, that "one great and largely uncharted area yet remains to be explored—the area of human consciousness."

Other men and women have overcome and are overcoming deeply rooted fears. You can do the same. It is simpler than you now imagine. The power of picturing yourself meeting a similar situation with greater fortitude will be realized by you as you practice it. Each time you repeat the picture, you will grow stronger in your resolution.

Do not try to force yourself to visualize these mental pictures. To try to force "fear thoughts" from your mind means that you are still not sure you can rid yourself of them. But, if you are convinced that your fears have no further hold upon you, you can quietly and firmly replace your fear pictures with pictures of yourself in full control of your emotions at all times.

Picture yourself as "boss" of every move, master of every situation!

An appeal to your reason will destroy fear. You would not knowingly tamper with a high-voltage wire. How infinitely more dangerous and destructive is your own subconscious, if wrongly used! And your fear thoughts are like an electric current, which, in time, will electrocute you, just as surely as a live wire, unless you learn to modify their intensity and eventually control them.

Man creates his own ills and spends a lifetime fighting them. You can cure most of your ills by eliminating fear. So here's to your liberation from the fears that have brought misery and heartache! As you turn the searchlight of your reason, your courage and your faith upon them, your fears will vanish into thin air, and you will attract the worthwhile things you have so long desired.

FEAR, THE PLAGUE OF HUMANITY, MUST BE OVERCOME

Today the world is fear-ridden. The threat of A-bombs and H-bombs, and who knows what other kinds of new and more destructive bombs, hangs over the globe. Under such horrific conditions, it is no wonder that the economic life of millions in all lands is in a delicate state of unbalance, and that fear of a third World War exists in the minds of great masses of people. Add to this the profound hates and resentments which seethe among various races, the fears and suspicions which tragically exist, and it requires great faith and courage for the individual to maintain the right mental attitude.

But, in the face of all this, it is absolutely imperative that you learn to control your emotions, your fears and worries, that you *picture* yourself receiving guidance and protection from the power within, so that you will be safe and secure no matter what may come to pass in the world at large, so that you can do all in your power to help extend your own influence for good as far as possible.

Be positive! Be courageous, believe, have faith, prepare your mind today, so that you can, to a greater degree, control your individual future.

THOUGHTS TO BUILD INTO YOUR LIFE

I realize that I fear only that which I have not conquered in myself.

To remove the hold that past fears have had upon me, I must recall them to mind and review them as I picture myself facing any similar experiences which may occur, in the way I should have done at the time.

Every time I feel the inclination to fear, I will stop the mental picture fear forces upon me and take conscious command of myself.

I will tell my subconscious mind to pay no attention to these fear pictures and will instantly erase them from my mind by visualizing myself courageously confronting the situation.

When I have convinced myself that my fears are, for the most part, foolish and serve no constructive purpose, they will tend to lose their hold upon me.

I will always remember the great statement: "Fear knocked on the door; Faith answered it—and there was nothing there!"

9

The Power of Faith and Self-confidence

Faith isn't just a word; it's a definite force, a vitalizer, an energizer, an organizer, a dynamizing influence that magnetizes conditions and sparks people into action!

The *doers* of the world are all *activated by* faith. *Faith is the mainspring of attainment. You must have it to achieve— to move yourself and move others!*

If you lack faith, you lack self-confidence. The two go hand in hand. With both faith and self-confidence working for you, you can't miss! Set your mind on some worthwhile goal; put the power of faith in yourself behind it, faith in the persons with whom you are associated, faith in "that something" within, which controls the destinies of everyone; cut out all negative thinking; proceed in a self-confident manner—and obstacles just have to begin disappearing!

Faith, as you know, is the keynote of all great religions. It's been expressed time and again by such spiritual leaders as Buddha, Confucius, Mohammed, Moses and Jesus and by many philosophers. It can be summed up in the one declaration: *"If you believe it, it's so!"*

Now, this statement isn't always literally true. Just believing in something, *anything*, doesn't make it a fact. I cringe when I hear some religious people using this statement, as if giving lip service to it would have the magical effect of some

88

word like "Abracadabra!" By "lip service," I mean using words with no conviction or feeling behind them, as though words, in themselves, had power. The days of Aladdin and his lamp are gone, and perhaps they never existed—so with the magic wand, the magic carpet and all of those things of fairy tale and legend. Entertaining and intriguing, perhaps, but no basis in fact, no reality.

There is *one* fact, however, you must always remember and it's an old spiritual admonition you've heard many times before:

FAITH WITHOUT WORKS IS DEAD!

Whether your belief or faith is based upon reality or not, nothing happens unless you put genuine effort behind what you desire.

There's absolutely no doubt about it, though—seeming miracles can be accomplished through proper exercise of faith. All big things are started by one person, one believer. It makes no difference where he got the idea originally. All great inventions are the outgrowth of the whole scheme of faith—belief in yourself, your ideas, your ability to put them over. All supersalesmen know this. They use the power. That's why they are supersalesmen of religions, commodities, projects. Every community drive, every forward movement, everything worthwhile, succeeds because some one person has faith, is the prime mover, the spark plug, the central fountain, and is able to sell what he has faith in to the multitudes—to pass faith on like a contagion. Think about that. Then think about it some more, and think of it again. Meditate on it, and you'll realize that every word is true!

You have faith in a religion, a commercial product, a community drive, because someone originally gave you faith in it. You accept certain people as authorities because you believe in them. What they tell you, you believe without question, and you take or buy what they offer you. That's faith.

Occasionally some person will mislead you and cause you to believe in something that isn't so; when you discover this, you are often bitter and disillusioned. You say, "I'll never believe in anyone again," but you will, because to believe is a fundamental trait of human nature. You instinctively want to believe in others and in yourself. This would be a terrible world if we couldn't trust anyone.

"Foghorn" Murphy, the famous umpire-baiter, said over the radio on Groucho Marx's *You Bet Your Life* show, that the "cheapest" thing a person could do was to be nice to other people, greet them with a smile and trust them—that this paid the biggest dividends. He's a thousand percent right: genuine faith in the other fellow always pays off. You may misplace your faith a few times, but this is a rarity. Most people make an extra effort to live up to your faith in them. They may fail others, even take advantage of them, but they are so appreciative of *your* faith that they won't let you down.

I've had men and women say to me: "What are you wasting time on that drunken, no-good deadbeat for? He can't be depended on. He'll steal you blind or take advantage of you at the first opportunity."

Well, I've placed my faith in hundreds and hundreds of men and women thus far, and I haven't yet been let down deliberately. Some of the folks I have trusted were just too weak to keep on an even keel, but they didn't go out to "take" me. They felt worse than I did about failing to live up to my estimation of them, and most of them have picked themselves up and have been trying, again and again. They know I still have faith in them—that I haven't condemned them, that I'm always willing to help, when and where I can. But they know, too, that it is basically up to them, that no person can be helped beyond a certain point, that they've got to do the job of getting back on their feet, themselves, through faith.

The power within cannot operate for you unless you have faith in it!

PUT YOUR BELIEF TO WORK!

Experience is the greatest and, at the same time, the severest teacher. Through experience, you *know* what you've done wrong; it beats in on you eventually. And after you know, you start to work setting yourself right, by realizing that you need some power greater than yourself to help straighten out your affairs and start you thinking right. So you discover "that something" within, and you say, "I believe!" And this sets up a magnetic current in you that commences to attract what you believe. And when you can feel and see coming *to* you the things that you have pictured through faith you say: "... *and it is so!*"

That's the process in a nutshell. It may not be religious in any orthodox or creedal sense, but it's spiritual, metaphysical. It's what the spiritual leaders of all time have been talking about, reduced to everyday language.

There are countless organized campaigns going on whose purpose is to get you to believe in this and that. Pause and think for a moment. What is propaganda, any kind of propaganda, the good and the bad? Often nothing more nor less than well-developed, ingenious plans to make you believe. You've seen it work during wartime and when the country or the world has been faced with great issues; if you're wide-awake to what is going on around you, you know that *today* it's being worked more than ever in every line of human endeavor, just as it was worked thousands of years ago, and as it will always work!

Take great care about what you are enticed to believe in. Be sure you are in unprejudiced, truthful possession of unaltered facts. If not, withhold judgment and don't permit your reason and intuition to be swept aside by convincing-sounding emotional appeals.

If when you are reading your newspaper, listening to the radio, viewing television, you keep in mind my theme, you will realize that all the speeches of your leaders, our great executives, coming to us with clock-like regularity, are being given with a purpose—to make us believe. These men know this. Even so: study everything that is said today, weigh both sides, draw your own conclusions, make up your mind as fairly and as unprejudicedly as you can, before you believe.

Every one of us, if put on the right track, can accomplish what he is after by keeping before him the declaration: "If you believe it, it's so," and by adopting the old adage: "Where there's a will, there's a way!"

In other words, get that willpower, that faith, that belief, working every minute of the day—twenty-four hours of the day, seven days a week, three hundred and sixty-five days a year. And I promise you, if you do, you will shoot ahead of people in the progress you make as rapidly as high-frequency electrical discharges oscillate through the ether!

Belief takes you where you want to go with the speed of jet propulsion. Doubt and disbelief take you just as fast in the opposite direction. Belief always magnetizes; disbelief demagnetizes.

You know something of the efficacy of prayer. What is prayer but the expression of a heartfelt, earnest, sincere want or desire? The Great Teacher said:

What things soever ye desire, when ye pray, believe that ye receive them, and ye shall have them.

And it's true! All of us know the effect of our own desires on ourselves and how events are influenced by great desires. Every economic change down through the centuries has been due to the desire of man to benefit himself. However,

92

we *must* believe, have faith. Otherwise, our innermost desires (prayers) become simply bursting bubbles.

The Great Teacher also said:

If thou canst believe, all things are possible to him that believeth.

You've heard all this before, but what have you done and what are you doing about it?

Belief—faith—is something that has to take hold of you after you take hold of it. It has to get down inside you and work from "within out." When you believe sufficiently in something, you bring it into existence in your mind. The creative power within creates it for you. Then it starts to work to duplicate it in your outer life. If you don't let your fears and worries and doubts change this picture, the original pattern that you gave your subconscious, there'll come a day when you'll see it materialized just as it once was in consciousness.

Believe—have faith—and as I have said, and say again to impress it indelibly upon your mind, "Anything you want can be yours!"

THE TREMENDOUS POWER OF FAITH!

You think faith isn't practical, that it can't do the things I claim for you? Here's a real-life demonstration of the workings of faith when the odds were *millions* to one against any power in the universe saving this man! (After I first reported this experience in the earlier book about TNT scores of men and women wrote to say that it had given their faith in themselves and the God Power within a terrific boost. I also had a letter from the man himself, referring to my account of his dramatic experience. In my reply I had the pleasure of telling him how much his example of faith had meant and would mean to countless others.)

Listen to this remarkable faith adventure, and prepare yourself for a great spiritual lift!

In September 1949, a nineteen-year-old Navy seaman, William Toles of Rochester, Michigan, was washed overboard from his carrier, without a lifejacket. It was four o'clock in the morning and he was far out to sea off the coast of Africa! No one saw him go overboard, and he knew when he hit the water that his chances of rescue were almost nil.

Instead of surrendering to wild panic, however, young Toles kicked off his dungarees, tied knots in the pants legs and used the seat of the pants to trap wind to inflate the legs, thus fashioning an improvised life jacket.

In his own story, Bill Toles says that he tried to use the enlisted man's practice of "not worrying about the future." He felt that he would be missed on shipboard at eight o'clock muster and that search planes would be sent to look for him, since he was on a warship which was steaming far off the courses of any regular liners.

Bill Toles had such control of himself that he even tried to sleep by resting his head against a leg of the inflated dungarees, but the big waves kept slapping him awake. Controlling his fears, this young Navy man called upon his faith in "that something"—the power of God within him—and repeated over and over: *Please, God—let me be rescued . . . Please, God—let me be rescued!*"

But when morning came and went and no planes appeared, Bill's spirits began to sink. He had become seasick from being flailed by the waves and from swallowing much water. Yet, never losing faith, he kept repeating his prayer: *"Please, God—let me be rescued!"*

At three that afternoon, after Bill Toles had been in the water *eleven* hours, he was sighted by sailors on the *Executor*, an American Export Lines freighter, who were amazed to discover a man in the ocean!

But, even more amazing . . . the captain of the freighter could not explain why he had switched his ship from its usual course off Africa to a Spanish course that intersected the Navy carrier's homebound route!

Had he not done so, he would not have passed within several hundred miles of the *one little spot* in the vast ocean where Bill Toles, with his unfaltering faith in God, was awaiting rescue!

Bill was in such good physical shape, after all he had gone through, that he climbed the ship's ladder of the *Executor* unassisted, and was toasted in champagne by the ship's crew!

But Bill Toles' first act was to thank God for answering his prayer.

Will you ever again doubt, in the face of such evidence, that "all things are possible to him that believeth"?

What *moved* the captain to change the course of his ship and go unerringly to this tiny spot in the millions of square miles of water, so that he could pick up a man who had faith that God would let him be rescued?

There is no limit to the reach of mind and spirit! How strong is your faith? It should be a great deal stronger after this. You will probably never be called upon to exercise such faith, under such testing, emergency conditions. It should therefore be easier for you to know and believe and to say "It is so," with respect to whatever you need in life.

Your ship will find you, one of these days, laden with all you desire, if you hold on to your faith.

Remember, I have said that the *doers* of the world are the believers. They believe in themselves, their own inner capacities and their ability to call upon the God Power within when needed. You have no way of knowing how deep *your* faith is until it has been tested.

A TEST OF FAITH

Quite some time ago, the great wire walker Blondin walked a wire rope stretched across the gorge below Niagara

Falls. It was a stupendous demonstration of balance and nerve control. The newspapers of the country were filled with the story. Headlines stated that Blondin had announced that on the following day he would push a man in a *wheelbarrow* across—on the same wire!

Few believed he could do it. But one man, by the name of Ruth, went up and down the streets of Niagara, offering to bet anyone that Blondin could and would accomplish this feat. The morning of the advertised performance, Mr. Ruth came face to face with the great Blondin himself. They were surrounded by a crowd of townspeople.

As Mr. Ruth shook Blondin's hand, he said: "Mr. Blondin—I'm one of your boosters. I believe you know your business. I believe you can do what you say. I believe you'll take your man across that gorge safely."

The great Blondin smiled. "It's indeed a pleasure to meet you, Mr. Ruth," he said. "I've been looking all day for a man like you. I want YOU to get into the wheelbarrow!"

They say that Mr. Ruth has never been seen since!

Well, let's leave Mr. Ruth out of this. Would *you* have gotten into that wheelbarrow? ONE man *did*—I've seen actual photographs of this spectacular event—and was taken across the gorge and *back* on that wire by the great Blondin, without mishap.

In any crisis in life, your *faith* must be equal to this crisis, or you will be unable to meet it. The power of TNT within you will be powerless to help you.

Your *faith* must be positive, expectant, unwavering and utterly sincere, or it will not energize "that something," the creative power within, which must be activated before what you have pictured can be attracted to you.

In an emergency, don't try to compel the answer to come to you at any specific time, because the God Consciousness does not operate within the time limitations of earth. Setting a time limit will make you tense and cause you to doubt that you will receive help in time.

All you have to do is maintain faith and confidence that help will come to you at the time you need it most. Such an attitude of mind will free the God-given creative power of any and all self-imposed limitations, enabling it to provide you with the aid and direction to meet your particular crisis.

Bill Toles didn't question that God knew His business when he kept repeating, with faith: "Please, God—let me be rescued!" He *knew*, he *believed*, and so it was!

Cast aside your doubts forever because:

If you believe it, it's so!

THOUGHTS TO BUILD INTO YOUR LIFE

I know I am powerless to achieve anything worthwhile without having faith in myself and in the power of God.

I also realize the truth of the often quoted declaration: "Faith without works is dead."

If I hope to achieve success, I must, in support of my faith, put forth every sincere and earnest effort toward my objectives.

The way to strengthen my faith is to study the courageous examples of others who have demonstrated faith in themselves under conditions of great emergency and to resolve to emulate them.

After picturing what I desire to accomplish or attain in life, it will help if I am able to say, with deep conviction: "I believe it—and it is so!"

10

The Power of Spoken and Written Words

You are living in an era of mechanized and electronically produced *sights* and *sounds!* The air around you is jammed with radio and television waves. And, if we had developed some way of detecting them, I wouldn't doubt that we would find we are also surrounded by thought, as well as television, images, since everything in the universe has a rate and character of vibration.

Think of all the radio and television stations that are continually broadcasting; then think of all the minds on this planet that are also functioning. In the form of energy or impulses, something we still do not understand is emanating from the field of human consciousness. It's good we are ordinarily insulated from consciously receiving all that is going on about us in the invisible. Fortunately, we are able to select what we want to take into our minds through our eyes and ears and other physical senses. But Science is hard at work, trying to invent gadgets that can reach our subconscious and impress us without our being aware of it, at the moment—like *subliminal* advertising.

You see, scientists now know that in a split second of time our eyes and ears record many sights and sounds that do not register, consciously. So people who want to sell us something figure that, if they can flash a picture or a few words across the television screens so fast that our conscious minds can't pick them up, they'll reach the subconscious and, through repetition, will get their ideas rooted there and influence our future desires and actions!

Pretty clever, eh what?

Buyacakeofsoap . . . buyacakeofsoap . . . cakeofsoap . . . cakeofsoap . . . sudsysoap . . . thatsthetradename . . . sudsysoap . . . sudsysoap . . . askforsudsysoap!

Fast-like—right past your eyes, and your subconscious is supposed to decipher this double-talk. I'm exaggerating and simplifying, of course. Subliminal advertising is much more subtle and high powered than this . . . and when fleeting pictures are added to the brain bombardment, you're really absorbing a barrage when you look and listen to commercials. The same goes for any ideas that are dished up to you, for one reason or another, through the various communication media. Your mind is reacting on conscious and subconscious levels to things that are happening in and around you at all times, awake and asleep. In the case of this advertising barrage, the intent is to influence you subconsciously so your conscious mind will set up no resistance at the start—and then, through repetition, to make these ideas eventually acceptable to your conscious self!

Now, if those who have something to sell are willing to put forth so great an effort to reach and persuade you, shouldn't you devote a few moments each day to deciding on your own what you want to do with your mind and your life?

What your eyes see and your ears hear, remember, if seen and heard often enough, make up a part of your existence. That's why scientists and advertisers have gone in for all manner of visual aids and recordings, aimed at impressing the minds of different groups and classes of people.

Some folks are influenced more by what they see, others by what they hear. It depends upon which sense they had developed the habit of utilizing most during childhood.

You may be on a car trip with someone and keep on noticing things, in passing, that the other person does not see. He or she is not trained in observation as you are, but might say to you: "Did you hear that?" And you may reply, "No, what?" There are varying degrees of sensitivity in sight and hearing.

"I was criticized so much when I was a child that I didn't want to hear what was said about me, so I don't hear now as well as I should," a man said to me.

"When I was a little girl," a woman related, "I saw something I shouldn't have seen. This shocked me so that ever since I have been afraid to use my eyes any more than I need to see what I have to see. I find that I am not paying attention to many things taking place around me because I inwardly feel it's none of my business and that I shouldn't be noticing them."

Inhibitions are one of the great self-inflicted plagues of the human race, but we all have our share, in one form or another. It is almost impossible not to have taken on some, during the growing-up process.

As adults, however, we should have the intelligence to recognize and to eliminate as many of these emotional tie-ups as possible, so we can be freed of their destructive influence over us.

Picturing the things you want to have and do in life is therefore a good method of crystallizing and pinpointing your desires so that your mind can better focus its attention upon them. And the more you can keep the picture or pictures before you, the more impressed the power within will be to help you materialize them.

PUT YOUR WORD PICTURES ON CARDS!
OR PUT THEM ON TAPE!

There are two powerful methods you can use to reinforce what you are picturing for yourself; they will help to keep your objectives uppermost in your thoughts.

1   Write a word picture on small cards, kept easily available so that you can refer to them, as frequently as possible.

2   If you have a tape recorder, speak your desires into it in the form of positive declarations or affirmations, so that you can play this back, at intervals or upon retiring, and receive the suggestive impact of your own voice.

You now have a *visual* as well as an *audible* aid working for you.

I don't mean you have to go around talking to yourself and writing yourself letters, but you get the idea! Don't make a fetish of it, don't overdo it, but it won't hurt to stick a card above the mirror to be seen in the morning, when you shave or fix your hair. Permit the details of your wishes, outlined on the card, to increase as you continue to develop the mental pictures.

Have another card convenient to look at while you eat your lunch, then your dinner. Use the cards again just before you go to sleep. Keep it up. Remember the unfailing power of *repetition!* There is no point, however, to writing down your wishes until you have determined that every single detail of what you want is to be photographed permanently in your thoughts, to stay there until it becomes a reality.

If what you are picturing for yourself is of a personal nature and there are people about who would not be in sympathy with your desires, or who would regard this practice as foolish, then keep your cards to yourself, and study them only when you have a spare moment and an opportunity for privacy.

The same applies to use of tape recordings in which you state your desires and ambitions. If there is a fault or habit you wish to overcome, a declaration in your own voice of your resolution to do away with it is powerful medicine. Your subconscious mind will drink it in and commence to set up roadblocks against this fault or habit. Every time you are tempted to fall back into the same practice, your subconscious will give you a mental nudge: "Hold on, here! You're not doing this any more—remember? That's a part of your past. It has no place in your present or future!"

WRITE IT DOWN OR SPEAK IT!

There is tremendous power in your spoken or written words. At least there can be if you really mean what you write and speak about yourself! You've got to *feel* it and you've got to *believe* that you've got what it takes to *earn* it.

You can't get something for nothing, and you've got to picture *something* before you can get *anything*. Things just don't happen out of clear skies, not even thunderstorms. The elements have got to be there or to be put there, to produce any happening.

Plant that picture in your mind! A perfectly detailed picture of the exact thing or things you wish. It won't hurt to picture more than one objective at a time, as long as they are not in conflict, and as long as you can picture them separately, one at a time. The creative power within can work on as many projects as you desire, and to which you can give your attention and efforts!

Write them down and speak them! Do everything possible to help externalize them, to bring them to pass in your outer world!

If it is increased sales you want, fix the exact amounts; if it's something you want the other fellow to do for you, the love of a woman or that of a man, a new suit of clothes or a new automobile—*write it down and speak it*. Tell yourself it is on the way to happening, that it has already come to pass in your mind. You just *know* you are going to attract what is needed to enable you to reach your goal!

It matters not whether you are a salesman, an executive, a mechanic, a writer, a housewife, an astronaut or whatever; whether you are after money, love, improvement in social position, in the legal or medical profession—it makes absolutely no difference. You have that same power in you, ready to bring you what you want. You can acquire every single thing you desire—a pair of shoes or a mansion. *You name it—write it down—speak it—and go to work on it!*

Opportunities are constantly flowing past you in the stream of life unless you reach out and grab them! If you don't know what you are looking for, how can you get it?

Every way you can express what you desire, in writing, in voice, in pictures, helps vitalize the creative power within and keeps your thoughts magnetized on the target.

Some men and women keep a large envelope labeled, "My Heart's Desires," in which they have recorded statements of what they want, of changes they wish to make in their lives, economically, personally, physically, mentally, spiritually. They put aside certain times during the day or evening when they can get off by themselves and reread and reflect upon the different written expressions of heartfelt desires. They also check each one and take inventory to see if they have made progress toward their respective goals. When they reach a certain objective, they mark the case "closed" and write on the card an expression of their thanks to the God Power within for helping them realize their dream. Then they go on to something else, constantly unfolding and developing. It is an endless, glorious, satisfying process!

If you are just starting, you will need to remake your thinking, eliminating many wrong thoughts and emotional reactions which are already in consciousness. To do this, it will be helpful to write down what you now realize *should* be your right attitude toward others, toward money, business, any and everything of importance that you have to deal with in your everyday life.

PICTURES WITH FEELINGS BEHIND THEM!

Think of pictures you have seen—paintings, photographs, landscapes—pictures of family and friends doing things, activities of various kinds. How many of these pictures do you remember? How many stand out in your memory and why? I'll tell you. Because something in those you remember caught your personal interest and held it; you saw something of yourself and your doings in them, you felt a kinship for some feature in them; they aroused your feelings; these pictures made such an impression on you that you never can or will forget them. In fact, these and other pictures you have seen, and countless pictures that you, yourself, have created in your imagination, are still making an impression on you in consciousness—where everything you have ever seen or heard or experienced continues to exist in picture form!

The feelings associated with these pictures are also influencing you. In fact, it is your feeling reaction to whatever has happened to you that influences you most of all. How deeply you feel about anything you desire, as I have said before and deliberately repeat again, determines how intensely the creative power within magnetizes conditions around you and attracts what you wish to you. Obviously, if you deeply fear something may happen to you, it will cause this creative power to work just as magnetically to attract what you fear to you.

Write fear out of your life by writing down affirmations of courage and faith and self-assurance. Speak them into your tape recorder and play them back. Read your words and listen to your voice! You *know* and *believe* good things are going to happen. You are ruling all fear and worry thoughts out of consciousness. You realize, if you permit them to remain, that they can only attract unhappy conditions.

Your *conscious* mind is a sieve and a filter at the same time. It takes everything that happens to you in this outer world into it and passes it on to the subconscious in the form of mental pictures. That's its normal, automatic process, unless you stop certain pictures and alter them, or don't allow what you recognize as a wrong picture to get through!

Now this thought may come to you as a shocker! The uncontrolled conscious mind of any individual is little more than an open sewer that takes in all manner of refuse and debris in the form of wrong thoughts and feelings, along with the good. Unless you stand guard over what you take in, there is no sifting, no filtering of the good from the bad. It all goes into your inner consciousness. And what goes in must eventually come out in the same form, or remain within to attract more of the same, because—let me say this again—*like always attracts like!*

You've heard of the "stream-of-consciousness." That's a pretty accurate description. Thoughts are streaming into and out of your mind all the time.

CONTROL THE NATURE OF YOUR PICTURES!

Warning: Don't let your stream of consciousness become any more polluted than it is! Put up your *filter screen!* Stop all fear and worry thoughts, all wrong emotional reactions, before they get into your inner consciousness where they can do you untold damage. Begin to screen out the wrong

105

thoughts and feelings that are already floating around in the stream of your subconscious. Bail them out. Get rid of them. Clear up this stream so it can reflect the good, clean thoughts you are now sending out upon the waters of your life experience.

Write down what you want to be. Speak it out loud. Write out of your life what you *don't* want to be! Tell yourself it no longer exists for you!

Constant practice of expressing yourself on paper and by voiced declarations will work wonders. Shortly, you can form the pictures at will, without the use of either cards or recordings of your voice unless you wish to continue because of the benefits you are receiving.

Don't be afraid of overdoing, or becoming excessive with your wishes and desires, because, as I have said before, you can have every single thing you wish, *within reason,* if you faithfully follow these techniques and are willing to put forth the effort necessary in support of what you are picturing for yourself!

When you visualize and keep the pictures firm and steady, action follows, because action, after all, is nothing more than *energized thought*.

Never lose your vision (your mental pictures) for, as King Solomon said nearly three thousand years ago: "Where there is no vision, the people perish."

Bear in mind that this whole theme is as old as man. I am merely giving you the message in words of today and outlining a simple system of mechanics that may be used by anyone.

As we all know, "The proof of the pudding is in the eating." And if you have any doubts as to whether or not I am giving you an exact science, *try* it! The automobile will begin to take shape, you will get the new shoes and the bricks of the mansion will fall into place as though a magical hand had touched them.

The weight of evidence is on the side of the thousands and thousands of happy, successful, healthy men and women who have already demonstrated and are demonstrating the working of "that something"—the God-given creative power —in their daily lives!

Keep a written record of the things you want, and check against it. You'll soon be checking the things off as you attain them.

Stop your daydreaming, eliminate your doubts, get busy, try writing down or speaking your desires, or both.

It *works!*

THOUGHTS TO BUILD INTO YOUR LIFE

I am aware of the power of suggestion and that organized efforts of advertisers and propagandists are being made to influence my desires, my opinions and my decisions.

A good practice is to put word pictures of what I desire to achieve on cards, to which I can refer at odd moments of the day and night, or to put these same word pictures on tape so they can be played back. In this way I will have visual as well as audible aids working for me.

I must control, at all times, the nature of my mental pictures, to prevent their being distorted or changed by fears and doubts or the possible adverse influence of others.

There is tremendous power in spoken and written words, when they are really meant and have strong feelings behind them.

107

11

The Power to Control Excessive Appetites

What kind of habits are you taking with you on the journey through life? Have you acquired some, such as smoking and drinking, that are giving you trouble? Have you developed the tendency, under everyday tensions, disappointments and frustrations, to smoke too much and drink too much?

A safe rule to follow is: *Moderation in all things.* If we could stay with this rule, we would encounter few serious difficulties in life. Unhappily, not too many of us can.

If your smoking or drinking habit, for example, has become excessive, you have a major problem on your hands. It is much easier to keep from developing a habit or an appetite for something than it is to eliminate it, once it gets a hold on you.

The method for overcoming a habit or an appetite that has become injurious to you is the same as applied to any established pattern of conduct but, because excessive smoking and drinking have moved into the forefront of physical health problems today, let's keep the focal point of attention on them.

How are habits or appetites formed?

Well, since you now know how your mind operates, you should be able to tell me. Every time you repeat an act, it is stored away in your mind in the form of a mental picture, along with the emotional reaction you had at the time. These feelings are strengthened and intensified by repetition. When you want to memorize something, for example, you repeat it over and over. The mind finally takes hold of it, and you can recite it almost backward and forward without thinking. It has become, in a way, a part of you.

A habit is nothing but a mental pattern—a way of doing something—that in time becomes as apparently natural to you as breathing. Once established, this habit, appetite or craving always stays with you, until and unless you do something to get rid of it.

Before an appetite is created, it has no emotional hold upon you. But by repeating a new experience (even one that isn't particularly pleasurable at the start) until you get accustomed to it, you may come to enjoy it and even look forward to experiencing the same kind of sensation again.

Many men and women have testified that they didn't find smoking or drinking at first appealing. But they kept on doing it because almost everyone else seemed to be enjoying it, and they eventually came to like it. In addition, few people derive pleasure out of doing things alone, and smoking and drinking are usually associated with sociability. This has led to the excuse that many men and women offer: "I don't especially care for smoking and drinking—but I just do it to be sociable."

How do you break a smoking or drinking habit? If you really want to stop, there is no halfway point. You can't succeed by just tapering off, cutting down so much a day until you are down to no smokes and no drinks. And you cannot win by saying to yourself: "I'm going to go without a smoke or a drink for a week, a month or a year."

A prominent businessman had become an alcoholic, a fact he did not wish to admit. He said to his friends: "I can quit anytime I want to quit, and to prove it to you, I am quitting right now and will not take even one drink for at least a year!"

True to his promise, this man, to the amazement of his friends, *did* stop. But, exactly on the date the year ended, he went on the biggest binge of his life. He had counted the days and the months, while this desire built up inside him, but his integrity—the habit he had established of keeping any promise he might make—had kept him from drinking until the time he had set was up! Then, released from the promise he had made himself and others, he cut loose!

A REVEALING CASE HISTORY

An attractive woman of about thirty-five, whom we will call Mrs. Gulley, attended one of my lectures in Los Angeles. At the finish, she stopped at the book table, picked up a copy of my book *Anyone Can Stop Drinking—Even You* and sought me out.

"Mr. Sherman," she said. "I'm terribly worried about my husband. He has been drinking too much lately but he won't go to a doctor or a psychiatrist or Alcoholics Anonymous. It makes him furious when I suggest that he do anything about it. Do you think, if I bought this book and took it home he would read it?"

"I very much doubt it," I said. "Anyone who has become a problem drinker usually won't listen to friends or loved ones, or admit that he has a problem. He is the last one to come to grips with reality and will put off facing the situation as long as he possibly can."

"Just the same," said Mrs. Gulley, "I'm taking this book home and leaving it around the house on the chance he'll be curious enough to have a look at it."

Two weeks later, I received a phone call from Mrs. Gulley.

"My husband has admitted that he's read some parts of

your book," she reported. "But he still made a fool of himself at a party last night. We had a talk this morning and I told him he simply *had* to do something about his drinking. He's dead set against Alcoholics Anonymous. He says he's *not* an alcoholic and he refuses to be linked up with that outfit. But I think I could get him to come to see you, since you're not a doctor or a psychiatrist. He seems to be scared of what they might say or do to him. Would you please let me bring him over to see you?"

That night, Mrs. Gulley appeared at my apartment with her husband. I liked him instantly. He had a warm, outgoing personality and a winning smile. As we shook hands, Mr. Gulley said to me: "Mr. Sherman, it's nice of you to see us, but I want to make it clear at the outset, I have no problem. I'm just here, at my wife's request, to ease her mind."

"Now, Fred," Mrs. Gulley tried to interpose. "You know that you. . . ."

"Oh, I drink a little too much occasionally," he continued. "Who doesn't? . . . And, when I do, Molly naturally gets a little upset. But I can stop any time I want. I'm definitely *not* an *alcoholic!*"

"I'm not saying that you are," I replied. "What is your profession?"

"I'm a missile designer," he said.

"That must be extremely exacting, high-pressure work these days," I surmised.

"It certainly is," he said. "The Government's pushing us. Several things have gone wrong. We've been working overtime."

"I presume many of your associates are under the same tensions?"

"They're most of them hard drinkers," volunteered Mrs. Gulley. "I tell Fred he just can't keep up with them."

"She's exaggerating," countered Mr. Gulley. "We have

to have some relaxation. A few drinks help loosen you up. There's nothing wrong with that."

"Nothing at all," I assured. "Social drinking—*drinking in moderation*—never hurt anyone."

"You see, dear," said Mr. Gulley, defensively. "Mr. Sherman agrees. There's nothing for you to worry about!"

"*Nothing*—when you come home drunk and start throwing things around and scare the children!" she retorted. "*Nothing*—when you even struck me last night and called me names!"

Mr. Gulley looked at her. "You didn't tell me that . . . I don't remember. . . ."

Mrs. Gulley held back the tears.

"Mr. Sherman, do you call that 'social drinking—drinking in moderation'? Do you think, as he says, I have nothing to worry about?"

It was a difficult moment.

"Mr. Gulley," I said on impulse, "I have made some records on the subject of alcoholism which are being used in a number of rehabilitation centers, hospitals and state institutions." I could see him stiffen. "Now, don't get the idea I am putting you in the category of an alcoholic. But I'd like, with your permission, to play the first side of record number one, and let you listen to it, and analyze yourself as I ask certain questions—and then *you* tell *me* where you would place yourself, as concerns your own drinking."

"Fair enough," nodded Mr. Gulley. He was seated on the davenport beside his wife, who studied him closely as the record started. Each question called for a direct answer. It had to be "yes" or "no."

> "*Are you drinking in the morning?*"
> "*Have you had blackouts?*"
> "*Are your sex relations unsatisfactory?*"

"Do you feel guilty about some things in your past?"

"Are you compelled to associate with people who offend, annoy or upset you?"

"Do you think you are in the wrong job?"

"Are you under mental and emotional pressure?"

"Has there been a tragedy you cannot wipe from your mind?"

"Do you see defects in yourself which have made you feel depressed?"

"Does jealousy of others disturb you?"

"Have money emergencies become unbearable?"

"Has the harmony of your home been jeopardized by the unwelcome presence of relatives?"

"Are you worried about losing your job? Your wife or husband? Anything and everything you hold dear?"

"Has betrayal by a friend or loved one completely unnerved you?"

"How many of these possible causes, and others not mentioned, have led to your excessive drinking?"

"How much of a problem do you think alcohol has now become to you?"

I stopped the record and looked at Mr. Gulley. He said nothing for a full minute, staring thoughtfully at the floor. Then he lifted his eyes.

"All right," he said. "So I've got a drink problem. I can see now where I've got to watch myself—got to cut down."

His wife started to speak, then bit her lips.

"Mr. Gulley," I said, quietly but frankly. "You are cold sober now. You are in full possession of yourself, mentally and emotionally. You have an important, fine-paying position, you still have a loving wife and children; you have the respect and regard of your friends and neighbors; you have, I am sure, money in the bank; you probably own your own home." He was nodding reflectively as I spoke. "You have now decided that you've got to watch yourself, got to cut down on your drinking. But is this *all* you have to do to protect the worthwhile things you have gained in life? May I ask you to do something for me?"

"What is it?" he asked guardedly.

"Will you just relax, and go back in your mind, and review the past six months—and tell me whether or not there has been an increase in the number of times when you have started out to do some social drinking and ended up drinking far too much?"

Mrs. Gulley nodded at me meaningfully. Her husband's face took on a troubled expression.

"Yes," he said, finally. "I'll have to admit—there have been more times."

"Now, Mr. Gulley," I said, "Will you please do one more thing for me? I would like for you to project yourself ahead in time, in your mind, one year from this present moment and, based upon the rate of increase in your excessive drinking that has occurred in the last six months, tell me where you think you will be a year from now?"

Again there was a period of silence, but little beads of perspiration began to appear on Mr. Gulley's forehead. He stirred uneasily.

"I—I guess," he said, reluctantly, "the problem *is* a little bigger than I thought. Maybe I *am* no longer able to control my drinking. Maybe it *has* been getting the best of me. Maybe I can't taper off. But you don't think it's gone so far—I'm still not an alcoholic?"

"Let's say you are certainly on the verge of alcoholism, if not an alcoholic," I said, "and by your own analysis."

"Okay, so I'll quit!" he said, impulsively. "I'll quit tonight. It's not worth it. I'll never take another drink!"

I looked him in the eyes. I had heard these assertions so many times before.

"You don't mean a word of it!" I said. "You have accepted the fact, intellectually, that you have a drinking problem, but you are already figuring how you can quit for awhile, just to prove you can do it, and then start drinking again— in moderation."

"You are reading my mind," said Mr. Gulley, a bit shame-facedly. "That's exactly what I was figuring."

"But you can't win," I replied. "Thousands of men and women, in the same condition you are in, thought they could do it. They failed and so will you, because you are no stronger or better than they are. Whether you yet realize it or not, a change in your body chemistry has occurred, and a taste of alcohol, beer, wine or whisky will awaken a compulsive urge. This, coupled with a mental or emotional disturbance, will lead to more excessive drinking, and you will find yourself worse off than you were before."

"You mean—from now on it isn't safe for me to take one sip of alcohol?"

"Not if you want to stay sober, not if you wish to retain your peace of mind, your health, your happiness, your position, your wife and family, your home, your bank account, all of which you can lose to drink in due course of time, unless you make the great decision now—*to stop drinking and stay stopped!*"

A different look came into Mr. Gulley's eyes. It reflected a deep inner feeling that had taken hold of him.

"I may need help," he said, "But I'm going to try—starting tonight."

"You may need to consult a doctor or a psychiatrist . . . and attendance at an Alcoholics Anonymous club can be of benefit," I suggested. "You will find that going without a drink is a day-to-day proposition. You probably have mental and emotional problems that need solving. They usually go hand in hand with excessive drinking. But you are in a much more fortunate position than many men and women who have let alcoholism ruin their lives almost completely, before trying to do something about it."

Mr. Gulley nodded appreciatively.

"I didn't think when I came here tonight, it was going to end up this way," he said. "I was so sure I didn't have a problem, so sure my wife was all wrong. This thing can become quite insidious, can't it? It can certainly fool you, creep up on you, in fact!"

"Yes," I agreed. "Any man or woman who begins drinking to excess should start questioning what is happening to them, but most of them don't, unhappily. Most of them make excuses, establish alibis, kid themselves into believing they can call a halt any time they wish, until they are hooked for good. Eventually, if they hope to escape from the ravages of alcoholism which, for them, has become a physical and mental illness, they must, somehow, develop the resolution to stop drinking, as you have now done—and to stick to it, every day, *for the rest of their lives!*"

Fred Gulley stuck to it. My meeting with him was over three years ago. Since then he has never taken another drink, and three of his associates, impressed by his example, have also quit drinking. They are all grateful that they stopped when they did, that they have profited by the experiences of others who did not stop, who made fun of them for stopping, for not being able to control their liquor—and who went beyond the point of no return in their own drinking and had a much longer, harder pull regaining their sobriety.

A certain percentage never make it. But there is always a chance that even the most depraved alcoholic can fight his way back with the help of a Higher Power within him and the help of the right physical and psychological treatments.

Alcoholism can be prevented much more easily than it can be cured or, one should say, *arrested*—because there is no known absolute cure for alcoholism.

The problem drinker who is approaching alcoholism

should be wise enough to stop before this stage has been reached. Danger signals are flashing each time a person drinks more than he intended to drink and becomes unaccountable for his actions, or starts having memory lapses, blacking out, preferring liquor to food at all times of the day and night.

The old saying, "An ounce of prevention is worth a pound of cure" aptly applies to the person who develops an excessive appetite for alcohol. That "ounce of prevention" is labeled "STOP," and it doesn't mean an ounce or even one drop or sip of alcohol in any form!

The average person is placed under too great a strain, once he has become a heavy smoker or drinker, to declare that he will never take another smoke or drink. Constantly in the company of others who are smoking and drinking, he is tempted many times a day to do likewise. It is easier to overcome an urge at the moment, than to say to one's self, "I am never, never going to taste a cigarette or a drink again."

Alcoholics have learned the hard way that they must pursue sobriety on a day-to-day basis. They thank God at the end of each day, that they have gone that day without a drink, and pray for the strength to live the next day in the same sober manner.

But to give up smoking or drinking, you must have an *incentive,* something to replace the desire to drink and to smoke. You must have an inner conviction that you will be better off freed of these habits, that smoking and drinking (in your case) can be and are harmful; that if not discontinued, they will keep you from attaining things in life which mean much more to you than any amount of smokes or drinks.

You are safe if you have proved to yourself and others that you have the willpower to practice everything in moderation, but not too many of us have, particularly where smoking and drinking are concerned.

Certainly I am not opposed to any individual choosing to do what he wishes to do in life. But it is painful to see some friends and relatives having a grim, losing struggle with such problems as excessive smoking and drinking.

Throughout the years, I have had so many men and women tell me they wish they had never started, but most of them seem to feel that it is too late to stop. They have resigned themselves to the habits and appetites because they are getting a measure of enjoyment from them that they do not want to give up, regardless of possible consequences. Their systems have developed a craving for the nicotine and the alcohol, and they feel nervous, irritable, jittery, and generally miserable without the "pacifying influence" of these supposed stimulants.

Those whom their doctors order to give up smoking and drinking because of afflictions, brought on in whole or in part by these habits, find it most difficult, if not impossible, to do so; some have said: "I would rather die than go without."

A friend, a lung cancer patient, persisted in taking drags on a cigarette each day, offering the excuse that he had the disease now and "a few puffs more won't hurt me one way or the other." A sad commentary on the power of a habit —once formed!

It is characteristic of human beings—you and me both —to think that what has happened to others is not going to happen to us. We have a tendency to laugh at statistics. We do not want to face the fact that, if we drive an automobile long enough, we are certain to have a few minor accidents and possibly a major one. The head-on collisions on the highway, running off the road over embankments, skidding into other cars, crashing because of blown tires and various other kinds of traffic mishaps may happen to other motorists but *we* are immune!

Other people may drink to excess and smoke to excess—but not us! We are *different!*

What does a smoker do when he is under emotional tension? He reaches for a cigarette.

What does a drinker do when he is emotionally disturbed? He reaches for a bottle.

We have grown up with a habit-formed dependence upon artificial stimulants as a means of controlling or calming our nerves. We have placed reliance, not upon our own normal, natural mental control of our bodies, but upon the habits of smoking and drinking to give us the "strength" to face situations in life! The more tension—the more we smoke and the more we drink!

You actually *do* in life what you want most to do; the strongest desire always wins out in the end. When you are convinced that you have more to gain by *not* smoking or drinking, by not indulging further in these habits—however pleasurable you may have come to feel them to be—you will have the *power within you to stop!*

Every time you are inclined to take a drink or a smoke, this more compelling desire will rise up in opposition. You will be reminded of your new and greater objectives, and you will put aside your urge to return to the old habits. Each time you are successful in turning down these urges, your *new habit patterns* of nonsmoking and/or nondrinking will become stronger and stronger until the day will come when you feel no greater mental and physical pangs at the thought of doing without smoking or drinking than one who has never indulged.

No person ever changes his conditions in life until he *changes his thinking.* There are many harmful habits besides smoking and drinking—excessive eating and excessive sexual indulgence, for example—but I have stressed these

119

two because, as I have said, they are among the most universal.

In any event, the same technique of thinking can be employed in bringing other habits under control or in ridding yourself of them entirely.

It is well for anyone with an admitted drinking problem to remember: *sobriety is just as close as the last drink*. Whoever has the courage and the resolution to face reality and make the decision to stop drinking, and who will stick to this decision day by day, can prevent for all time any further inroads of alcoholism.

If you are a moderate, controlled social drinker, you have no problem—until and unless control is lost and excessive drinking begins. This is the time to take immediate inventory should what I have said in this chapter have any relation to you. Delay can mean ultimate ruination and degradation. Millions of alcoholics bear grim testimony to the fact that "they waited too long" and "acted too late."

THOUGHTS TO BUILD INTO YOUR LIFE

The safest rule to follow in life is "Moderation in all things." I will encounter few difficulties so long as I follow it.

It would be wise for me to take a personal inventory and if I find that I have developed excessive habits in drinking, smoking or some other personal pattern of conduct—I shall take whatever course of action may be necessary to regain control of myself.

I must make sure that I am not kidding myself; that I do not accept the often false assurance that, "I can stop doing whatever I am doing any time I want to do it."

THE POWER TO CONTROL EXCESSIVE APPETITES

I realize that I endeavor to do what I desire most in life; the strongest desire always wins out in the end.

For my own protection I must, therefore, check my desires and acquired appetites and habits to see if they need correction or elimination before they ruin my health and my reputation.

12

The Power of Extrasensory Perception

Extrasensory perception, or ESP, is a phrase known throughout the world now, but it did not exist a comparatively few years ago.

It was coined by Dr. J. B. Rhine, head of the Parapsychology Department at Duke University, pioneer investigator of the higher powers of the mind, to describe perceptive faculties beyond the reach of the five physical senses.

In the old days before Science took a serious interest in ESP, it was called "psychic phenomena." This might mean *telepathy*—the ability of one mind to communicate directly with another mind, unlimited by time or space; or *precognition*—the ability to foresee the future; or *psychometry*—the ability to tell many things about a person just by touching an object or piece of clothing belonging to this person, or *automatic writing*—the ability to let your arm and hand be controlled by your subconscious mind, writing messages or inspirational material that you cannot produce with your conscious mind; or *trance mediumship*—the ability to put your physical body to sleep and let alleged higher intelligences use the body as an instrument through which to communicate; or *psycho-kinesis*—the power of mind over matter in its ability to influence objects such as dice; or *astral projection*—the ability to leave the physical body at times and travel through space in a purportedly higher vibrating body form, ordinarily invisible to the physical eyesight; or, *materialization*—the alleged ability of some spirits of departed loved ones or friends to temporarily take on physical form once more, through drawing on the "psychic forces" of a medium, and being thus enabled to recognizably appear to living mortals. In my book, *How to Make ESP Work for You*, I explain these various types of "psychic phenomena" in greater detail.

Up to now you may have been crediting to *Intuition* the different hunches and premonitions you have had in either a waking or dream state. This is as good a name as any but we now know that it has been your ESP faculties that have provided you with guidance and protection. There have been thousands upon thousands of well-witnessed cases of men, women and children who have received ESP impressions. Let me cite a few examples:

EXAMPLE 1:

Dr. Hubert Pearce, then pastor of the Methodist Church in Heber Springs, Arkansas, had just received his winter's supply of coal, which had been piled at one side of the furnace. While down in the basement with his janitor, he was suddenly struck with a powerful mental urge.

Turning to the janitor, he said: "I want you to begin, at once, shoveling all this coal over to the other side of the furnace!" The janitor looked at him, amazed. "Doctor, you must be out of your mind! That's at least a day's job of hard work! If you wanted the coal on *that* side of the furnace, why didn't you say so at the time it was brought in?"

Doctor Pearce shook his head. "I didn't feel this way

about it, then," he said, a bit bewildered at his own sense of urgency. "But it's got to be done. I can't explain why—*it has to be done!*"

A protesting janitor went to work. When he was half through shifting this pile of coal, he made a discovery.

"Doctor!" he called. "Come down here, *quick!* Come here and see what I found!"

When Doctor Pearce arrived, he saw his janitor pointing excitedly at a large piece of coal, in which was imbedded *a stick of dynamite!*

"Well, now, I am relieved in my mind," said the doctor. "*Something* told me there was a danger of some kind in that pile of coal. If that dynamite hadn't been detected, it could have been shoveled into the furnace and badly damaged our church!"

Remarkable, you say? Yes, to anyone who is not yet aware of the existence of these higher sensory powers, but Doctor Pearce happened to have been an "old hand" at demonstrating these inner faculties. In his college days at Duke University, he had served as a "guinea pig" in telepathic experiments conducted by Doctor Rhine's parapsychology laboratory. And he was the *first* person who ever received twenty-five straight correct impressions of the ESP card symbols—a cross, circle, square, star and wavy line as mentally transmitted to him by Dr. J. Gaither Pratt! The possibilities of a successful chance recording in such a phenomenal run of telepathic hits are so astronomical as to be ruled out entirely. But Doctor Pearce scored consistently well above chance in these now-famous tests, which were continued with him for some time.

To me, most interesting of all was the fact that these extrasensory abilities have remained with Doctor Pearce in his later years, to the point in this related instance, wherein he was made aware of impending danger!

EXAMPLE 2:

A woman wrote me recently to report an unusual impression she had received when she awakened on the morning that she and her husband and children had planned to leave on a vacation trip. The time for departure had been set, but this woman begged her husband to delay the start an hour or two, because she felt, if they left at the hour scheduled, they would become involved in a serious automobile accident.

"Honey, if we don't leave on time we can't make our destination before dark," her husband reasoned. "You've never felt this way before. If you dreamed something was going to happen, forget it. There's nothing to this dream stuff. Let's get going!"

"You probably think I've suddenly gone crazy," said his wife, "but I'm not going with you unless you lock all the doors in the car!"

"But we've *never* locked our car doors!" said her husband. "Okay—if you insist. To me, this is all a lot of foolishness!"

The vacation-bound family left home at the appointed time. After a half hour en route, they were rounding a turn in the road when an oncoming car, traveling at high speed, rounded this same curve *on the wrong side of the road!*

To avoid a head-on collision, the woman's husband swerved his car off the highway and down an embankment. After the car turned over twice, its downward roll was stopped by a tree. Because the doors of the car were locked, father, mother and two children were bounced around inside the car but not thrown out. They all escaped with minor bumps and bruises. But for this premonition, this mental warning, some of them might well have been killed or seriously injured.

Important observation: Do you see now WHY this

woman's extrasensory faculties tried to get her to *change the time of departure*? If they had waited even half an hour before taking off on their trip, the car with this reckless driver at the wheel would have passed this point in the highway and they would not have been in the area of potential danger! Somehow, there was a part of this woman's mind that could sense what was coming toward her in time!

Whenever you get a strange, inexplicable feeling or hunch of this kind, it pays to give attention to it!

EXAMPLE 3:

A Mrs. Sharpe owned and operated a telephone-answering service for doctors. She had long possessed a working knowledge of ESP. One night around midnight, a new girl who had been hired to take and transmit messages for the physicians called Mrs. Sharpe in a state of panic.

"I'm sorry to have to disturb you," she said, "but an emergency call has come in for Doctor Thomas and I can't reach him at any of the numbers he has listed. The hospital tells me they must get hold of him in the next half hour or one of his patients may die!'"

"Now, settle down and take it easy," instructed Mrs. Sharpe. "Get those fear thoughts out of your mind. If you can't reach Doctor Thomas by phone, you'll have to make contact with him *telepathically!*"

"What's that?" said the girl, bewildered, "What did you say?"

"I said," repeated Mrs. Sharpe, "that you and I are going to concentrate our minds on Doctor Thomas. We are not going to try to imagine where he is or what he is doing at this hour. But our minds, if directed to him wherever he is, will find him. I want you to sit quietly and say mentally, with me: "Doctor Thomas—I need you! . . . Doctor Thomas, you are wanted! . . . Phone your answering service right away! Phone your answering service at once!"

There was an almost stunned silence on the phone.

"Are you working with me?" demanded Mrs. Sharpe. "Whether you believe this or not, you know there is an urgent need for Doctor Thomas. You feel it! Now put those feelings behind your thoughts as I am doing. Do this, and you'll hear from Doctor Thomas in the next ten or twenty minutes . . . twenty at the outside! I've done this before and it works! Now, take it on faith, and do as I say!"

The girl operator complied. Silently, the two women sat, one at home in bed, and the other at the switchboard in the telephone answering service office, concentrating, sending out the "mental call" for Doctor Thomas.

Within *ten* minutes, Doctor Thomas phoned in from a friend's home to ask: "I just happened to think, you don't know where I am. *Is there any message for me?*"

Incredible? No, in time to come, humanity-at-large will acquire this extension of awareness and use this *sixth sense* as naturally as we now rely upon our five physical senses!

Recently, Everett F. Dagle, Research Engineer for the U.S. Air Force Cambridge Research Laboratories in Bedford, Massachusetts, was quoted as making this statement at an Aero-Medical Association convention in San Francisco:

> I feel that the time has come for us to examine ESP and the higher mental processes as possible communication aids to our astronauts who, in the foreseeable future, will be voyaging perhaps more than one hundred million miles into space. On such long, solitary trips, they will be surrounded for weeks or months by a black void, broken only by pinpoints of light from distant stars. Far removed from the gravitational pull of the earth, they might find it difficult to maintain their mental and emotional stability, unless they had some developed ability or assurance that

they could still make almost instant connection with their home planet. That far away in space, it would require nine minutes for a radio message to reach the earth and nine more minutes for a reply to be received—eighteen minutes in all, which could seem an eternity to an astronaut about to panic. But, if it were possible to develop the faculty of telepathy so that astronauts could send and receive thought messages, and if they could make instantaneous, feeling contact with a sensitized human creature on earth—it might help them maintain their sanity.

TIME AND SPACE NO BARRIERS

Of course, ESP is not developed to the point wherein communication of this kind is conceivable for some time to come. But when I acted as receiver in the now-historic experiments in long-distance telepathy with Sir Hubert Wilkins (recounted in our book *Thoughts Through Space*), it was demonstrated that I was able to record mental impressions from his mind when we were separated by some two to three thousand miles, with an approximately 70 percent accuracy. Sir Hubert Wilkins was then conducting search flights in the area of the North Pole for a period of five months, looking for a crew of Russian fliers who had been forced down on an attempt to fly nonstop to the United States. I was living in New York City, and three nights a week from 11:30 to 12 midnight Eastern Standard Time by prearrangement, I sat in my study in my New York apartment and concentrated on Wilkins. Wilkins, allowing for the difference in time as he flew farther north, would get off by himself and relive and review the outstanding things that had happened to him that day. It was my assignment to try to intercept and record his thoughts. The experiments were observed by scientists, who testified to their authenticity by affidavit.

The fact that time and space apparently constitute no

barrier to the transmission and reception of thought, and the fact that Wilkins and I were able to communicate over a distance of two to three thousand miles, would suggest that, when more is learned about the performance of telepathy, it will be no more difficult to reach the mind of an astronaut a hundred million miles from earth than it is to reach a mind in the next room.

MANY SCIENTISTS STILL SKEPTICAL

Anyone who has been a pioneer investigator and experimenter in the field of ESP has not had an easy road. Many scientists still reject Telepathy or ESP as something that just cannot happen; that exists within the realm of imagination, coincidence, guess-work, or just plain trickery and charlatanism.

I can understand the reluctance of such scientists to go on record in support of ESP, even when, at times, confronted with actual evidence that it *has* taken place. One of the reasons is that no one who practices genuine telepathy or any phase of ESP can ever guarantee, as yet, 100 percent results. There is always a possible margin of error, impressions that are wholly or partially inaccurate or off the target.

This is usually due to the emotional factor and the suggestive interference of the conscious mind which is limited by the five physical senses. When an impression is received from the subconscious, where the Extrasensory faculties exist, the conscious mind will produce, if permitted, a wall of doubt. It will try to argue with you about a hunch or a premonition or a feeling to do or *not* to do something on the basis that there is no provable reason for accepting such an impression as having any validity in fact.

Scientists, however, have had to base *their* observations

and findings upon what they regard as demonstrable facts —which can be repeated successfully, over and over again.

CHALLENGES TO ESP

Some months ago, when I was in Los Angeles and New York, I appeared on many radio and television shows in the interest of my new book: *How to Make ESP Work for You.* During the telecasts, I made it a point to state that I did not give public demonstrations of telepathy or any phase of ESP. I explained that if I attempted to get impressions and succeeded, too many people in the audience would consider it a trick or a prearranged stunt. If I failed in an effort to perform telepathy, many in the audience would conclude there was nothing to ESP.

The public-at-large knows little about these higher powers of the mind beyond possessing a curious interest in the subject. Such persons could not be expected to comprehend the difficulties involved in trying to demonstrate ESP before a radio microphone or a television camera.

But, despite my declaration, there were times when attempts were made to deliberately put me *on the spot.* There was one time on the coast when I was interviewed by the charming and vivacious Pamela Mason, first on television, then on radio.

Following my television appearance, Miss Mason invited me to come to her home on a Sunday morning, to record a taped interview for her forty-five minute radio program. When I arrived, I was ushered into a private room and seated beside a tape recorder and told that Miss Mason would be in shortly. When she finally breezed in, in her cheery, business-like manner, she greeted: "Hello, Mr. Sherman—what have I been doing today?"

My mind did a quick turn and I answered. "Well, my over-all impression is *legal!*"

"Oh, is that so?" was Miss Mason's rejoinder, and with no further comment, she sat down beside her tape recorder, flipped it on, and began the interview!

Half way through, during which time she had asked me how telepathy is performed and many other questions pertaining to different aspects of ESP, she suddenly said: "You know, Mr. Sherman, you were right about my being engaged in *legal* matters today. As a matter of fact, I have been with my lawyer for several hours this morning. Tell me—*what does he look like?*"

I hesitated for a moment, and then answered: "He is a comparatively young man, a trifle stout, with dark hair and eyes, and he appears to be wearing dark glasses!"

"Well, that is very good!" replied Miss Mason. "Very accurate, in fact. My lawyer *does* look like that—and he was wearing dark glasses this morning for the *first* time. I think, like most lawyers, he is trying to hide from someone or some thing." Then she went on to say: "I confess, Mr. Sherman, I was trying to trick you. I was picturing in my mind, before I asked you the question, a little stoop-shouldered, old man, with gray hair and so on, exactly the opposite of the way my lawyer looks. Tell me—why didn't you get the impression of *him?*"

"Because, Miss Mason," I answered, "you had vividly impressed in your subconscious mind the mental image of how your lawyer actually looked . . . and it was much more strongly etched in your consciousness than the image of the fictitious attorney you had imagined!"

"Well!" said Miss Mason, "I guess there *is* something to telepathy!"

Under these circumstances, I was fortunate to have received correct impressions. The proof is contained in the tape recording of this program. I could as easily have failed and what could or would Miss Mason have said then? And what position would this have placed me in?

ANOTHER DIFFICULT PUBLIC TEST

There was another time in New York, when I was interviewed for two hours on Radio Station WINS, on the program called "CONTACT." The interviewer was a man named Stan Bernard and he had as "the devil's advocate," to cross-examine me, past president of the Magicians' Society, Melburn Christopher.

The interview was from ten to twelve midnight, and Mr. Christopher announced at the outset that he was a disbeliever in ESP. It is not my temperament to try to convince announced skeptics, nor do I get mentally or emotionally upset by their questioning. Occasionally the going gets pretty rough and amounts to needling, and I sometimes think that my questioners hope they can get me nettled so that verbal fireworks might ensue. In this case, having explained to Mr. Bernard prior to the broadcast that I did not publicly demonstrate ESP, Mr. Christopher, nevertheless, produced a sealed package and challenged me to tell him what was inside it.

He said, "Mr. Sherman, in your ESP book, you tell of a number of incidents wherein you were able to successfully divine what was contained in sealed envelopes. I would like to have you see if you can get a correct impression of what this packet contains."

Remember, this was a live broadcast. I looked at Mr. Bernard who said something about not knowing that Mr. Christopher was going to present this test. Mr. Christopher insisted, however, that I would certainly not mind a little experiment like this—as though it would be just as easy for me to perform telepathy, at any time, as it would have been for him to perform a feat of magic.

To refuse to accept this challenge, I instantly realized, would never be understood by a large segment of the listening audience. The inference was plain that Mr. Christopher did not believe in telepathy or psychometry, as this specific phase of ESP is called, and my failure to describe the nature of the object in the sealed package would not only cast doubt upon whatever ESP ability I might have been credited with possessing, but would prove his contention to have been right.

I pointed out that no one professing to perform genuine telepathy or psychometry could guarantee in advance that he could secure above-chance results. There was no time to explain why this is true. I sat back and held the packet in my hands. As I made my mind receptive, the first impression that hit me was the negative mental atmosphere with which I was surrounded. Both Bernard and Christopher had their eyes and minds focused upon me.

Silence is not golden on radio. Seconds were ticking off. Under the pressure of time, with the awareness that thousands of minds were tuned in on this program, it required unusual mental discipline not to panic or freeze.

After about thirty seconds, I said I could not get an impression of the nature of the object . . . but my predominant impression was one of *"severe emotional disturbance and death."*

"Is this all you can get?" said Christopher.

I took an additional moment.

"This is all," I said, "But I repeat—I get a strong feeling of emotional disturbance and death."

Mr. Christopher then handed to Mr. Bernard a sealed envelope with the following printed statement on his personal stationery (which I have in my files).

CHRISTOPHER

This leather cover was used by my friend, Dr. Jacob Daley in his "coins through hand" trick.

The two magic words on it, in plain English mean "cockroach."

Dr. Daley died at the end of a sleight-of-hand performance at the New York Art Directors Club on East 40th Street, February 17, 1954.

He was a physician and plastic surgeon by profession, magic was his hobby.

When Mr. Bernard had completed the reading of this statement, I said:

"Will you please re-read the paragraph telling of Dr. Daley's death?"

I then reminded Bernard and Christopher that while I had not been successful in describing the object, I had accurately picked up the most powerful emotional impression concerned with Dr. Daley—*his death experience.*

To which Mr. Christopher replied: "Anyone could have guessed that."

So you see, you cannot win, in any attempted public demonstration in the face of such an attitude. This is what has made it so difficult for those who *do* possess a measure of genuine telepathic or ESP ability. It has required quite a degree of courage to face skepticism, indifference, and often charges of self-delusion or fraud, from many quarters.

But the day is fast approaching, in my opinion, when we are going to discover techniques that will enable us to bring our higher mental processes under conscious will, control and direction. As of now, I am sure that many of you, reading these pages, have had spontaneous manifestations of ESP—what you have called "hunches" or "premonitions"—strong feelings to do or not to do something, prophetic dreams or visions, the ability to foresee the future. Perhaps you may have seen apparitions, heard voices, had the sensation or experience of leaving your physical body. Or, you may have found yourself in a trance condition, temporarily under the apparent influence or control of an entity. Or, you may have observed the movement of a physical object untouched by any human hand. And some of you may feel that you have received messages from those who have passed away, or, on occasion, are aware of their presence.

All of these experiences have to do with one or more phases of what used to be called, as I have stated, "Psychic phenomena."

If you have had experiences such as I have described, I wish you would write to me in care of ESP Research Associates Foundation, 1750 Tower Building, Little Rock, Arkansas, and give me a detailed case history report. We are making a study of these spontaneous occurrences and you may make a valuable contribution to the increasing knowledge concerning these higher powers of the mind.

IS ESP EVIL OR GOOD?

I am often asked, "Can ESP be used for evil purposes as well as good?"

Yes, unfortunately, it can. Like everything else God has given us, as creatures of free will and free choice, we can make good or evil use of it. Witness Atomic power—the good uses that can be made of it—and yet, how man is converting this stupendous power into weapons of destruction! I am sure that the Russians are investigating ESP, with no spiritual purposes in mind. If they can discover how to use ESP to serve their own ends against us—they will do it. They have been exploring the theory that thoughts are electro-magnetic in nature—that they travel in thought waves or impulses. They speculate if it were possible to determine the frequency of brain waves and if these brain waves could be electronically reproduced and magnified or amplified—to a great intensity—might it be possible to electronically beam these waves into mass consciousness—and mesmerize or influence entire populations of people?

Sound fantastic? Like Science Fiction? If your existence

on this earth dates back to the turn of the century, you wouldn't have believed then that man could ever fly—much less takeoff for the moon and distant planets. Today you had best keep an open mind—prepared for anything to happen!

HELPFUL USES OF ESP

My interest in the development of ESP has always been to make good and constructive use of it. Of course, with my background of experience in ESP, I am having adventures, from time to time, and I am occasionally called in to see if I can be of help in determining what has happened in connection with some tragedy.

I do not seek such assignments, because they are difficult, often unpleasant and very emotionally taxing; I make no claim to infallibility. But I had an experience in recent months which is well documented. The recounting of it may give you added assurance that these higher powers of mind *do* work and for helpful purposes. But, because of the personal nature of some of the impressions received, I am not mentioning, by name, the parties involved.

On February 9, 1965, out of a clear sky, I received a long distance phone call at my town house in Mountain View, Arkansas, from a Mrs. P. of South Bend, Indiana.

She said she had been referred to me by Dr. Karlis Osis, Research Director for the American Society for Psychical Research, in New York. He had suggested that I might be able to help in determining, through extrasensory perception, what had happened to a private plane, containing her son-in-law, daughter and grandson, and a hired pilot, which had disappeared after take-off, the night of January 3rd, from St. Petersburg, Florida, airport.

Mrs. P. stated that, thus far, more than a month after the plane's disappearance, no trace of it had been found. Without waiting for Mrs. P. to give me any further information on the phone, I broke in on her to say that I had an immediate impression the plane was down in the *water*.

Mrs. P. said that this was impossible—that the Air Force and Civil Air Patrol told her no pilot with any flight experience would ever take a single engine plane over water, especially at night.

Despite this statement by Mrs. P. I insisted that I mentally saw the plane *in the water*. I felt it would be found soon . . . by a fisherman in a boat.

I also felt that her son-in-law and daughter had had an argument before take-off. She had not wanted to go—had wanted to wait until morning. I went on to say that I felt her son-in-law was in personal trouble of some kind—of a serious nature.

Mrs. P. said she wouldn't know about that, but would it help if she sent me some articles of clothing worn by her daughter and grandson, so I could get further impressions? I said: "It might."

Consequently, she mailed to me on February 9th a glove belonging to her daughter, and a knit cap of her grandson's, together with pictures of them and the son-in-law. These were received by me on February 11th. She also sent me, at that time, a photostatic copy of a report made to her by the Eastern Rescue Center of the U.S. Air Force, elements of the State Police and Civil Air Patrol, which stated that the search for the missing Piper Comanche plane, N7418P, had involved some 900 people and over 500 aircraft, which had flown a total of some 1100 hours over a wide land area without finding any evidence of the plane's whereabouts, or of what might have happened.

For the first time, I realized the enormity of the effort that had already been made to locate the missing plane—a search that had now been abandoned.

My Conscious mind tried to tell me that I must be wrong

in the feeling I had expressed to Mrs. P. over the phone—
that the plane had crashed in the water instead of on land,
as these reports all surmised. There was no reference of any
possibility of the plane having landed in the water, and no
search had been made over water.

It was Saturday, February 13th, before I felt I should
undertake this *psychometric* assignment. I wanted to be sure
I wasn't *forcing*, because when you try to force, you often
activate your imagination.

Frankly, I had picked up such a disturbed impression
about the son-in-law during my phone conversation with
Mrs. P. that I was reluctant to get back into this *vibration*.

But, when I held the glove and knitted cap in my hands,
I felt, more strongly than before, that my *original* impressions had been right.

As I began to *see* and *feel* conditions, in my mind, I wrote
them down, as follows:

> *I go off to the left from line of flight, losing altitude, as
> though weighted down. I am headed roughly in direction
> of Tallahassee, Florida, about a mile high. I am in trouble
> —some instrumentation . . . some engine . . . which is miss-
> ing. I have to get down. There is some panic—argument
> between hired pilot and son-in-law. Daughter and grand-
> son in rear two seats. Some change in flight plans . . . .*
>
> *Son-in-law not in good humor before flight take-off. In-
> sistent about something . . . desire to get somewhere . . . not
> wait till morning . . . reason for hiring pilot for night fly-
> ing. Daughter unhappy about something, tight-lipped, tries
> to reassure son, has not wanted to go. Weather apparently
> contributing factor.*
>
> *Off course . . . body of water . . . swampy area . . . forced
> landing . . . searching for level area . . . dark, shadowy out-
> lines . . . ends in crash . . . plane disappears in water . . .
> does not burn . . . but not visible from air.*
>
> *Soggy soil, water . . . shattering impact . . . Not all killed
> outright but all badly injured . . . not able to escape from*

138

*wreckage . . . boy's body may have been thrown clear . . .
all bodies not together . . . .*

Feel search to left of flight pattern, as far off as forty to
fifty *miles, criss-crossing over area where plane might land
in* water, *might yield results. I have no knowledge of
nature of this country and do not want to know, because
this would color impressions should any of them prove to
be valid.*

*There seems to be a raised land area to the right of
where plane is down. It may have just cleared this in falling. Thickly wooded land area not far from water . . . possibly soggy section.*

I believe fragments of plane and bodies will be found in
water *when weather conditions are better . . . possibly by
fisherman in boat . . .*

*Your son-in-law impresses me as what might be termed
a 'smooth operator.' I feel, unhappily, there were at least
two other women in his life, and one who had some claim
on him. He was an attractive personality, a persuasive individual, who could charm and impress people. He had
extravagant tastes and ambitions—some grandiose and beyond his business capacity. But he had been able to cover
up well and to gain confidence of many. Not all bad, by
any means. But, at time of tragic death, under pressure,
trying to straighten things out. I get a disturbed feeling in
pit of stomach, as if I can hardly stand inner feelings, as if
I'm being hemmed in by events of my own making.*

*Hope these feelings are wrong because I sense wonder-
ment and concern of daughter, who does not seem to
understand or comprehend. At any rate, this overall sensation is strangely mixed up. To this extent, the pilot, who
has been hired to make this flight, is a victim of circumstances—the desire to make the night flight—the trouble
that develops in the air.*

*I cannot tell whether any drinking has entered into this
or not . . . .*

*Your daughter is an idealistic person, interested in
home-making, hopeful of satisfying the demands of an er-
ratic but brilliant husband. The boy is a wonderful, outgoing personality, who takes more after his mother.*

I wish I could be more definite in pin-pointing the location of the crashed plane, but I feel it will be found in time . . . .

The missing plane *was* found, three days later, on February 16th, by a *fisherman* from Hudson, Florida, who came upon the wreckage at a 12-foot depth of water in the Gulf of Mexico—some *forty* miles off to the left of flight pattern from the take-off point of the St. Petersburg-Clearwater Airport, in exact accordance with my impressions, about five miles off shore.

The plane was in fragments, as reported later by the Civil Aeronautics Board. Most of the disintegrated fuselage and small sections of both wings were recovered within an area fifty feet in diameter. Only parts of the bodies were found, again as I had forecast.

On April 26th, Mrs. P. sent me an affidavit, testifying to the correctness of these impressions, which reads as follows:

To Whom It May Concern:
On February 9th, I called Mr. Harold Sherman asking his help in locating my daughter, grandson and son-in-law who were missing after leaving St. Petersburg, Florida, the night of January 3rd, in their own plane, along with a pilot hired by my son-in-law.

After talking to Mr. Sherman, I sent him a glove belonging to my daughter and a little knit cap of my grandson's. Mr. Sherman said he had a very troubled feeling about my son-in-law, and that he was sure the plane would be found in water, and by a fisherman.

I remember disagreeing with him about finding them in the water, as so many pilots who talked with us, said they felt certain that any pilot with any experience would never go over water in a single engine plane, especially at night.

On February 17th, the pilot's wife, with whom I had kept close contact, phoned me to say that the Chief Pilot at St. Petersburg had informed her the plane and the remains had been found in the Gulf.

140

I chartered a plane and flew to Tampa. On the morning of February 18th, I met the pilot's wife at the dock where they brought in pieces of the plane. At this time they had not recovered any of the remains. *The Chief Pilot had been mistaken.*

I identified the plane and my children's clothing, and my daughter's bill-fold. They did not find anything of my son-in-law's, that I saw, not even clothing.

They found a man's shoe with the *foot in it.* But, according to the size of the shoe, it was decided that it was the pilot's.

When I had talked with Mr. Sherman by phone, he said he felt that all the bodies would not be recovered at once. I strongly believe that my son-in-law jumped or was thrown out before the plane crashed as there was absolutely nothing of his to identify.

The pilot's wife told me she went to the airport at St. Petersburg, from which her husband and our family took off, on the night of January 3rd, after they were reported missing. She learned then that there had been quite a discussion between my daughter and my son-in-law, that my daughter did not want to go until morning, and that, finally, my son-in-law said he would hire a pilot to fly them.

So, Mr. Sherman was right about the argument that took place between my son-in-law and daughter. He was also right about a fisherman who would find the plane.

I would further like to state that Mr. Sherman, if he had lived with and known our children, could not have described them any more clearly. He told me things I would not have believed about my son-in-law had not people very closely linked with him, told me.

My daughter was very young, 24 years old, hated any argument, and never raised her voice. She was the perfect mother. I know that she knew nothing of my son-in-law's previous character. I believe that after he married her, he did try very hard to be a decent person. *He certainly had us all fooled.*

I am forwarding a copy of this report to Dr. Karlis Osis, American Society for Psychical Research, who referred Mr. Sherman to me.

Later, on July 1st, Mrs. P. wrote me again, forwarding a copy of the Civil Aeronautic Board's full report on the finding of the missing plane. It contains the entire history of the fatal flight, from its point of take-off to its point of recovery in the ocean, with a listing of all parts of the plane recovered, as well as bodies, the full weather report of that night, and a statement that the plane was flying at a height of between 5,000 and 6,000 feet when last heard from.

In my recorded impressions, I stated that I felt that the plane, when trouble developed, was about *a mile high*.

Mrs. P. enclosed a letter she had written to Dr. Osis, in which she again repeated:

> I called Mr. Sherman after you gave me his name and telephone number. The first time I talked with him, he told me he was *positive* they would be found *very soon*. He said he was *very positive* that they would be found in the *water* . . . that he had a *very disturbed feeling* about my son-in-law. He said he was sure the plane had turned back. I promised him an item that belonged to my children, which I mailed out that day.
>
> When I talked to Mr. Sherman, I did not feel too encouraged as several pilots had told me they were sure the plane was not in the gulf because they would not go over water in a single engine plane.
>
> *Everything that Mr. Sherman said in his report was exactly correct.*
>
> After I received his report, I started checking into my son-in-law's background and would prefer not to put in writing what I came up with.
>
> I am so appreciative of all you people have done for me. If there is anything that I can ever do for any of you, please let me know.
>
> (Signed) Mrs. P.

You naturally want to know how my mind was able to go back in time and see and feel all these events in detail. I wish I had a specific explanation but no one yet understands how these Extrasensory faculties obtain information. However, there must be a vibratory record kept by Nature of everything that happens to everyone in what might be called "the mental ether," for want of any way to describe it, and which it is possible to tune in on when you fix your mind upon a certain person.

The son-in-law was dead when the impressions came to me of the past life he had lived. But I had to be getting these accurate impressions from *some* source. Believers in so-called "spirit communication" might suggest that I had obtained this information from his entity in the "after life." However, I rule this out as highly improbable. I was conscious of no contact with any of the four who had met death in this plane crash. As I fixed my mind's attention upon them and let myself "wonder" what had happened to them, this knowledge simply "flowed into my mind" in the form of mental images and strong feelings, which I had to interpret in my own words. This was not telepathy. Two other phases of ESP were involved, known as *clairvoyance* and *psychometry*.

No one knew, at the time I was called in, that the plane had crashed in the water, so this fact was not in anyone's consciousness. My mind then, reaching out through time and space, somehow sensed what had taken place at a distance and I was enabled to mentally see the fragments of the plane in the water. Before any articles were sent me belonging to the daughter and grandson, I had already, as reported, received the impression of the son-in-law's duplicity and an argument he had had with the daughter before takeoff. For me to be able to sense this information it had to be existent in some form. Where and in what state is one of the great mysteries that those making a study of Extrasensory Perception are trying to unravel.

In Psychometry, it is believed that everything you do is recorded or imprinted on every object or piece of clothing associated with you, and that a sensitized individual can tune in on these "vibrations" by contact with the article. Under these conditions, he can sense things that have happened to you, particularly highly emotionalized experiences. These impressions come to him in the form of fleeting mental images, strong feelings or "knowing" sensations— all of which he must interpret in his own words.

Fortunately, since my impressions in this case turned out to be so accurate, they were well witnessed. Copies of my impressions were in the hands of Mrs. P. and Dr. Osis before either had any knowledge or confirmation of the many details I had recorded.

Most scientists are not ready to concede that any sensitive can obtain such personal and intimate knowledge through extrasensory perception as I was able to receive in the case just reported. They will not accept that extrasensory perception is possible at all. I invite those interested, however, to check this case in its every particular. Mrs. P. has volunteered her cooperation and I am sure that Dr. Osis will aid in any investigation of all the facts and conditions involved.

One of the country's top psychiatrists and researchers in ESP, said to me in discussing this case:

> It does not require a thousand cases to prove the existence of extrasensory perception. It just requires one empirical case, thoroughly investigated by scientists, and if it defies explanation on any known physical basis, if it cannot be explained except by extrasensory perception, then, whether we can yet understand how these phenomena are accomplished, we must accept them as fact.
>
> Personally, I have maintained a neutral "pro" and "con" position—but, if ESP is one day proved to my satisfaction, I will have to throw my text books away and start in all over again!"

Of course, such a drastic action would not be necessary, but scientists *will* have to widen their horizons, abandon their closed minds, and accept that man's consciousness possesses non-physical properties of awareness far beyond the five senses.

What I have been able to demonstrate, under observed conditions, at various times in my life, other sensitives have also been able to do. I cannot be certain of one hundred percent results each time I try, nor can anyone else. We do not as yet know enough about these higher faculties to bring them under that effective and dependable control. But further research and experimentation, I am confident, will give us, in time, this facility.

My ESP Research Associates Foundation is at present receiving hundreds of reports of ESP experiences from men and women in all walks of life. It makes no difference what their religious convictions are or whether or not they have believed ESP to be possible. These experiences are coming to them, anyway, under stressful emotional or receptive conditions. This is clear indication that these extrasensory powers exist in everyone's mind and only are awaiting recognition and development.

YOU CAN DEVELOP YOUR ESP POWERS

In my book, *How to Make ESP Work for You,* I describe the techniques by which these different phases of ESP are performed. Greatly simplified, this is the basic method by which you can develop the sensitized ability to transmit and receive impressions:

1. You must be able to completely relax your physical body.
2. With your body relaxed, you must then make your conscious mind passive.
3. Now turn the attention of your conscious mind inward —and let yourself imagine that you are looking, with

your mind's eye, upon a blank, white motion picture screen, stretched across the dark room of your inner consciousness.

4. Hold this mental image of a blank picture screen as a focalizing point, as you concentrate upon the person from whom you wish to receive impressions.

5. Do not try to force impressions to come. Remain relaxed in body and mind. Let yourself have an expectant feeling, in the faith that you will be able to see images cross the mental screen, from the mind of the friend or loved one who is acting as *sender*.

6. The first image or feeling that comes to you, if you are actually in attunement, is apt to be the correct one. Write it down at once . . . then relax, awaiting the next impression, and so on.

With practice, you may well be surprised at the number of correct hits you will make.

In sending, the same method is used, in preparing the mind. Then, when ready to send, create mental pictures of whatever you wish to try to transmit, or develop strong feelings about the experience or thought you want to impart. Continue holding these impressions, while willing them to the *receiver*.

It is my conviction that we all possess these higher sensory powers in dormant or partially developed form and that when we give recognition to them—when we have faith that these powers can and will serve us—they commence to function for us! Doubt and disbelief keep these powers from manifesting just as definitely as doubt and disbelief prevent your creative powers of mind from operating in and through you. These extrasensory faculties are all part of the same great power. A sudden, inexplicable impulse or urge to do or not to do is your intuition. These extrasensory perceptions are trying to deliver a message to you.

146

Occasionally, you will receive an impression or a mental picture flash of a future event, some happening that is coming toward you in time. Don't let your conscious mind argue you out of it if you have a strong conviction that this premonitory impression is genuine.

I believe that man has it in his power to create his ôwn future to a very large degree. The more he can learn to develop and depend upon his higher powers of mind and his intuitive faculties, and to follow his genuine hunches and premonitions, the more he can avoid unhappy experiences and attract good happenings to him.

YOU NEED TO KNOW MORE ABOUT
YOUR SUBCONSCIOUS!

Before you can accomplish what you want to achieve in and through your own mind, you must know more about the workings of your subconscious. There is a great deal of mystery associated with its functioning, and many scientists, physicians, biologists, anthropologists, psychologists, psychiatrists and other authorities are trying to gain more light on what happens in the deep recesses of man's brain.

They've now discovered that great sections of man's brain can be removed without impairing his consciousness or his intelligence. You've heard of the electroencephalograph, that sensitized apparatus that detects and records brain waves. I've recently learned of a new instrument, now under development, by which the positive and negative currents in every organ of the body can be charted to determine their "electrical" state of health.

You see, the physical body isn't the grossly material organism we once thought it was. It is now referred to as an "electrochemical machine" of great sensitivity. A few years ago, scientists thought that the so-called soul was a part of the body and died with the body. Today, they are not so sure.

In fact, many scientists have concluded that intelligence —consciousness—may not be a part of the body at all, but simply manifests *through* the body. Picture yourself, then, as a temporary tenant, living in your own wonderful house of flesh, gaining experience and evolving your soul or consciousness through this experience while here, finally departing from this house when it has become impaired or outworn its usefulness.

Fantastic? Nothing is fantastic in this Space Age. What the mind of man can conceive, the mind of man can achieve. Man has desired *immortality* for as long as man has had conscious existence. He has dreamed and written and sung of a "life to come" in his religions, his philosophies, his songs and his personal aspirations. Now it is becoming apparent that man has been intuitively sensing "a land beyond the reach of the five physical senses," no less real than the world he is now in, a land that awaits his coming after the change called "death."

As you develop your own awareness, you, too, will become conscious of an increasingly positive conviction that "this life is not all"; that it is "just the beginning" of a continuously unfolding experience and adventure in God's great universe!

The key to this deeper understanding of self and your true relationship to the God consciousness within is to be found in your developed control and direction of the subconscious part of you.

How much do you know about your subconscious mind? Do you know it's the most remarkable mechanism in the universe? Perhaps *mechanism* isn't the right word, but you've got to call it something. It operates with the precision of a watch *if* you properly direct it. If you had a servant who trusted you implicitly and followed your every order right down to the minutest detail, brought you everything you thought you wanted, whether it was good or bad for you, you would have a small sample of what your subconscious does.

If I seem to be repeating myself in different ways, that's exactly what I am doing. It's highly important that you have a true and understandable knowledge of just how your subconscious functions. It stores away for your future use all the mental pictures and feelings of experiences you have had. How you feel about anybody or anything is filed in your subconscious. Your fears and worries and hates and prejudices are all there, along with your good thoughts. When you think good thoughts, you tune in on other good thoughts of the same nature that are already on file. If you like somebody today and nothing happens to change this regard, you will like him more tomorrow, because each day's feelings about that person are added to the feelings of the day before. Repetition is a tremendous force.

Start doing things a certain way, and you'll keep on doing them that way unless you change your mind or something happens to make you act differently. You form a groove in your mind like the groove in a phonograph record, but the groove doesn't have to stay that way. You can make a new groove anytime you wish, because you are a creature of free will and free choice and your subconscious mind is always controlled and directed by your conscious desires and decisions.

Your subconscious is a vast reservoir of knowledge that you have acquired through past experience and education and reflective thinking. It also possesses knowledge that it brings through your intuitive faculties—your *extrasensory perceptive* powers—because a part of your subconscious is not limited by time or space. It is a powerhouse of energy that reaches out into the universe around you and brings you an awareness of things that you could never get through your conscious mind alone.

Just how your subconscious does all this, no one knows,

but scientists are gathering plenty of proof that you are a powerful sending and receiving station with what amounts to a universal hookup. You can be put in contact with just about anybody or anything you want. Of course, not many of us are developed to the point where we can direct these higher powers so as to communicate *consciously* with the physical, mental, psychic and, spiritual worlds. According to many investigators, we may one day be able to tune in, not only on the present, but the past and future as well.

YOUR BODY IS A REFLECTOR OF YOUR THOUGHT!

Your subconscious is the one part of you that never sleeps. If it ever lay down on the job, your body would stop functioning, for it contains the miraculous intelligence that keeps your heart beating, your lungs breathing, your stomach digesting whatever you eat (and don't think that doesn't take some real doing, at times!). Every organ of your body, including the functioning of your five physical senses, is regulated by your subconscious, and if you don't interfere with its control by throwing a monkey wrench into your subconscious machinery in the form of fear or worry, your heart never skips a beat, you breathe without thinking about it and you never know that your stomach is digesting your food. But start getting upset about something, making your body tense—and watch your heart start to palpitate, notice how your breath gets short and how you don't feel like eating because your stomach is tied in a knot. Perhaps you even become sick to your stomach.

This ought to teach you to take care of your thinking and let your subconscious take care of your body. If you tell your subconscious that you are upset, your subconscious *has* to tell your body the same thing, because your body—the house you live in—is just a reflection of your thought. You can't simply *say* that you feel well, if you feel ill.

Give your subconscious mind a problem to work on just before you go to sleep. Have faith that this higher intelligence within you can and will solve this problem. Forget about it, and in the morning, as like as not, you'll wake up with the answer or know what to do to get the answer. The more you practice giving your subconscious jobs to do, the more it will carry the ball for you. It's the most willing servant you will ever have! It doesn't mind how much you pile on the work, how many problems you hand it, how many desires or goals you are carrying in consciousness at one time. Remember: your subconscious is not limited in its operation, except as you limit it by your limited thinking.

This amazing subconscious possesses a power that, for want of any better way to describe it, is *magnetic*. It seems to magnetize conditions around you the moment you give it a clear picture of what you desire. And it commences attracting everything you need, even the people you need to meet, to help you get what you are after.

Things start happening so naturally that you often don't realize your subconscious mind is doing it for you. It is using all of its powers—on the physical, mental and spiritual aspects of your life—and focusing these powers on your objective.

You can't fail if you properly instruct your subconscious and maintain your faith in the wonder-working God Power within. But the most mysterious of all your subconscious workings is—you guessed it—what science calls its "extrasensory faculties."

There are those who believe that they can, on occasion, communicate through mind with dear ones who have gone on. Why not? If human beings survive death and can communicate, mind to mind, while on earth, they should still be able to reach us *through mind* when we have developed our powers of sensitivity highly enough . . . or in our dreams, when the conscious mind is blanked out and we are in the subconscious realm, not bounded by time or space!

Arthur Godfrey, in an issue of that fine little inspirational magazine *Guideposts,* tells of a "psychic experience" of his own:

> It was in 1923. I was stationed on board a Navy destroyer —in charge of radio communications. I had knocked around a lot since I had left home. The years and life had not been too kind but the Navy had been a sanctuary, the only security I had known for a long time. One day, I fell asleep in my bunk and dreamed.
>
> My Dad—I had not seen him for years—suddenly walked into the room. He offered his hand, saying, "So long, kid!" I answered, "So long, Dad." I said some kind of prayer; It wasn't eloquent but it came from the heart.
>
> I never saw him again. When I woke up, my buddies told me that at the exact time while I was asleep, the wires from shore hummed the news of my Dad's death.
>
> Don't tell me about science and its exact explanation of everything. Some things are bigger. God is the difference. He gets around.

Yes, God *is* the difference—the God Power within. But it's up to you to develop this power and learn to use it in your everyday life. Train yourself to follow your hunches, the guidance you receive from the impressions that come to you. If you believe in your higher powers, if you have faith they will operate for you, they will! And, once you have had any experiences of your own, similar to those I have described in this chapter, you will never doubt again!

THOUGHTS TO BUILD INTO YOUR LIFE

Every individual possesses the faculty of extrasensory perception, often referred to as a "Sixth Sense," which functions beyond the reach of the five physical senses.

When an impression is spontaneously received by the average person, it is usually described as a hunch or premonition—a strong feeling to do or not to do something.

The best known phase of ESP is Telepathy— mind-to-mind communication. There is a technique for sending and receiving thoughts which can be learned. It may eventually be developed and used by astronauts, as a means of keeping in "feeling contact" with fellow human senders and receivers on earth.

This "telepathic outer space" communication is perhaps for the far future, but the fact that man possesses these higher powers of mind indicates that he has a destiny beyond this life.

It also suggests that man is connected in some still inexplainable way, through the Cosmic Consciousness level of his inner mind, with what must be termed the God Presence.

These ESP powers manifest through Intuition, and serve to guide and protect those who develop their inner awareness.

I accept on faith that this guidance and protection can be mine as I make my mind receptive to the functioning of ESP in and through me.

13

The Power of Personality

One of your most priceless possessions *is*—or *can* be—your *personality!*

Given the right expression of your personality, you have, through it, the power not only to move "mountains" but to move people.

You can move people to like you, to believe in you, to help you, to work with you, to give you their love and friendship, their understanding and loyalty—all in return for what you *are*, what you *represent*, to them.

When you learn how to *project* your personality, this power to move "mountains" (any obstacles or difficulties in life) and move people becomes the most dynamic, the most magnetic, the most appealing of all powers.

No human ever succeeds in a big way until and unless he has learned to release the charm and force of his personality.

What *is* personality?

It is YOU in outward expression, what you reflect in everything you do and say. It is the look in your eye, the tone of your voice, the way you walk and gesture and smile, the way you dress and work and play, the interests you have in life, your talents and abilities, your attitude toward yourself and others!

It is all this and more. It is your capacity to express yourself in a manner distinctively different from any other person who has ever lived. You are *you* and no one else can ever be you—in just the individual and characteristic way that you are *you*.

There may be those who will resemble you in appearance, in physical stature and likeness, but even they are not exact replicas, because Nature creates no doubles, no precise duplicates in all the universe!

You are different, you exist in a mould that is all your own, and it is up to you to make the best and the most of what you brought into this world that represents YOU.

All right, let's face it. Just what *did* you bring into the world? Are you residing in a physical form that may be adjudged short or tall, thin or fat, handsome or ugly? Are you handicapped in any way? Do you find yourself inhibited through some past experiences, fearful, self-conscious, lacking in self-confidence, unable to express your real self as you would like? Do you feel you are not getting from life what you should?

If you do, consider what others have done with their lives, how they have managed to project their personalities above and beyond all seeming obstacles and limitations.

Have you stopped to realize the degree to which you have been influenced by others, the impact that their personalities have had upon you?

Think of the many and varied impressions that all whom you have met and with whom you have associated have made upon you! In addition, you have been equally affected by the lives, the thoughts and deeds of personalities whom you have never met and never will meet. Some of these personalities may not have lived in your time, but their projection of what they came into this life to do and to say has been so powerful that it continues to exist and have its influence in the minds of men—your own included.

Consider the stupendous influence that Jesus and his

philosophy have had upon human consciousness! You must also credit such great minds and personalities as Confucius, Lao-Tse, Mohammed, Buddha, Zoroaster, Moses, Plato, Aristotle, Socrates, Aquinas, Descartes, Spinoza, Kant and numerous others with having left lasting marks upon untold millions of their fellow humans.

Likewise, for contrast, you have only to survey past history to have evidence of the *devastating effect* personalities such as Genghis Khan, Julius Caesar, Hannibal, Alexander, Napoleon, Kaiser Wilhelm, Hitler, Mussolini, Stalin and countless other tyrants and dictators have had upon the world.

Your personality can thus be a power for good or evil, depending upon how you express it. Your influence in life will be in proportion to the magnitude of your accomplishment in whatever field of activity you choose.

You may not be destined to be a leader, to be a big name in your community, state or nation. Comparatively few of us rise to the heights of a Winston Churchill, a Dwight Eisenhower or a Mahatma Gandhi, but we still possess the opportunity to express ourselves successfully and happily where we are, rendering a valued and often-appreciated service to all who come within the reach of our personality.

This should be your objective in life—to serve as best you can, where you are, in the faith that a job well done and a life well lived will bring its commensurate rewards to you and your loved ones.

And who knows? A top performance on your part in any profession or activity may lead to top recognition. You *could* be unknown today and a big name tomorrow. This is not impossible. Contained within every personality is the potentiality for *greatness*. Are you willing to dig your uranium mine, to refine the gold that is in you, to polish and strengthen your weaknesses, to invest the time and effort necessary to get the maximum returns out of yourself?

Go back in the lives of any of today's outstanding men and women, to the time before they had become "somebodies." What do you find?—A certain amount of talent and ability in process of development. Personality defects, no doubt. Lack of experience and preparation. A will, nonetheless, to "get there"—to overcome whatever obstacles they were facing—to profit by their mistakes, to rise above failures and disappointments.

No one ever succeeds to high attainment who has not had to meet adversity, to surmount periods of ill health or accident, to correct negative mental and emotional reactions to life happenings.

You achieve through overcoming. This is the path of progress. The way may seem hard, but the goal is sure if you meet and pass your tests, as they arise.

Everything in life is comparative. When you start sympathizing with yourself and indulging in self-pity, you can always look around, if you can make yourself take a detached point of view, and find people much worse off than you are.

The development of your personality and its most appealing all-round expression is not an overnight achievement. It's the little things you do each day, the way you are reacting, mentally and emotionally, to what is happening, how you feel toward others, what you think about yourself and those with whom you come in contact—all these experiences are doing something to you which are reflected in and through your individual way of expressing yourself.

HOW TO CAPITALIZE ON YOUR LIABILITIES

You think, for instance, Nature has handed you a bad deal because you may consider yourself homely and odd looking. *If you accept this "image" of yourself, you will project it to others.* But what did *Phyllis Diller* do when she took stock of herself in the mirror some years ago? She saw the figure of a woman that, as she might say, would stop two grandfather clocks. She had everything that the Elizabeth Taylors of the world didn't have, and all in the wrong places. How could she ever make anything out of her funny face, her wild-looking hair, her un-Sophia Loren body? What *did* she possess that she might capitalize upon? Her family of five "kids" could use a little more of that "green stuff" if there was something she could hit upon to do to help bring it in.

Well, it didn't do any good to keep on accenting the *negative*. She decided she would have to make a study of herself and see if she could come up with some merchandisable ideas. As an aid to taking personal inventory, Phyllis Diller went to the library and brought home two books. She told me herself, that they were *The Magic of Believing* by Claude Bristol, and the original edition of *TNT The Power Within You,* credited to Bristol and Sherman.

"These books emphasized that you had to get the 'right picture' of yourself before you could get anywhere," said Phyllis, "and that started me thinking—wondering what kind of a picture or image other people had of me? Fortunately, I was born with a contagious sense of humor and the ability to laugh at myself. I recalled that whenever I would go out to a party or for a social evening with friends, that I would *kill* them by the way I would tell stories of what had been happening to me and the kids. I just unconsciously put expression into whatever I was doing or saying, screwing my face up and going through different contortions with my eyes and hair and hands. Well, let's face it—I use every part of my body when I am in action and now that I'm on the stage, I dress this frame in as outlandish gowns as I can find or have made.

"But going back to the year BPD—*Before Phyllis Diller* —the idea hit me that, instead of entertaining friends and neighbors for free, why not assemble some of these wise-cracks I had been tossing off and test them against a *paying* audience to see if they would laugh just as hard at my goofy antics? I got my chance at a little, roadside nightclub —and everyone howled. From that time on, I just seemed to explode into the 'big time' and people have been howling at me ever since. Every time I appear on television or on stage, they start laughing even before I open my big mouth. As for me, *I* laugh, as they say, all the way to the bank!"

Phyllis frankly attributes her rise from "Gags to riches," to the day she looked in the mirror and decided, since she wasn't going to be beautiful, she had better concentrate on developing a good personality. The image she accepted and then created and perfected, has now been projected into the minds and hearts of millions whose spirits have been lifted and lightened by her hilarious take-offs on herself.

Today, having become one of the world's funniest comediennes, Phyllis Diller states that she conscientiously follows her "visualizing program." *She takes time each day to "picture what she wants" and checks different achievements off as they come to pass.*

What Phyllis Diller has done with what nature gave her, plus the appreciation of her own creative ingenuity, should inspire you to discover your perhaps still hidden possibilities. Find a way to turn your supposed liabilities into assets.

THE VALUE OF NOT TAKING YOURSELF TOO SERIOUSLY

When you can manage to laugh at yourself, even in adverse or disappointing and disillusioning moments, you are on the way out of your difficulties. But if you take yourself and what happens to you too seriously, you tend to "freeze" yourself to that situation, and you attract more unhappy experiences of like nature.

Of course, you cannot, nor would you care to be another Phyllis Diller or a Groucho Marx. They have personalities peculiar to themselves and bodies, of which they have made the most, entirely unlike yours.

In the case of Groucho, his small stature and facial features would not ordinarily have attracted attention had he not converted them into assets. Once he did this, he hit the top in his field of comedy, along with his equally crazy Marx brothers. When their highly successful combination broke up, Groucho continued on his own in television, projecting his personality so effectively that, once exposed to him, you always carry a mental image in your mind as "the man with the cigar and the elevator eyebrows." You can "bet your life" that you even feel better thinking of him, because he suggests humor as you see him, in your mind's eye, wiggling his eyebrows and his cigar at you. In other words, Groucho "sends you" every time you recall his image to your mind.

HELEN KELLER, AN ALL-TIME EXAMPLE

If you were totally blind and deaf from infancy, what chance would you have given yourself of ever amounting to anything? This happened, as you know, to Helen Keller. You may have seen the stage play and the motion picture on her life; how she was a headstrong, rebellious child, lost in a dark inner world, lacking any rational awareness of the world outside herself. But a woman, Miss Anna Sullivan, who herself had been partially blind since a young girl, came into her life at the age of eight. Miss Sullivan became Helen Keller's teacher and, after years of instructive devotion, reached her defiant pupil through love and laboriously taught her a finger language, and later the Braille system of reading. As time went on, the developing Helen was seized with the urge to learn to talk. In a remarkably short period she became able to speak intelligibly, sensing how to enunciate by feeling the vocal cords of her teacher! At the age of twenty, she entered Radcliffe College, from which she was graduated after a four-year course. Then she entered public life as a writer and lecturer, her heroic overcoming of her physical disabilities proving a tremendous inspiration to countless young and older people who had considered themselves hopelessly handicapped.

In Boston, on one of the first occasions when she spoke in public, she astounded a group of physicians by addressing them fluently in three different languages!

Never undersell the possibilities you possess for development of your inner resources, for expressing your personality in such a manner as to command the respect and regard and affection of others!

Where *you* are, you aren't starting with half the handicaps with which other men and women have had to contend. It helps mightily to realize this fact. Quite naturally, you either consciously or unconsciously wish to emulate the appealing qualities you see in others. You are therefore building into your own life experiences a little of what others mean to you. And, in like manner, the mental images you are projecting of yourself are finding lodgment in the minds of loved ones, friends and acquaintances and making their influence felt to a greater or lesser degree.

Are you satisfied with the *image* of yourself that you are projecting? If not, decide what you need to do to improve it.

It will help to do some more reviewing of well-known personalities whose mental images exist in your subconscious. Study their effect on you as you recall such individuals as:

Bernard Baruch! What kind of mental picture does he bring to mind? A man with a white shock of hair, eyeglasses and a hearing aid, seated upon a bench in Central Park, New York, meditating upon world problems? This is the image the press has given you of him—the "elder statesman," the "advisor and confidant of Presidents," a "clear thinker on national and international problems." You have probably accepted these "facts" about him, and you experience a feeling of security as you think of him. You have faith you can depend pretty much on his judgment in world affairs.

What comes to mind as you focus your thoughts upon *Dwight D. Eisenhower?* Don't you see a balding man with a broad grin, wearing a white cap, swinging a golf club? You perhaps sense, also, a certain earnestness and ruggedness which gives you a feeling of assurance that here is a man who is sincerely trying to do the best he knows how for the country. You may have been opposed to Eisenhower politically and may or may not have approved his administration of his high office, but you have doubtless pretty much accepted this impression of him—as he has consciously or unconsciously projected it.

When your mind turns to thoughts of beautiful women (if you are a member of the male sex) the chances are that it still produces some luscious mental images of the late *Marilyn Monroe*. This depends, of course, on whether or not your preference is for blondes or brunettes and whether or not what Marilyn Monroe possessed was and *is* your particular "dish." You may not be especially impressed by intellect in the glamorous female images you have stored in your subconscious for future reference, but you *are* mightily impressed by *form* and the personality behind the form. The women whose shapes have the greatest sex appeal for you dwell most vividly and alluringly in your consciousness. The same applies to men, the symbols of attractive masculinity, when the mental viewer is a woman.

All personalities are registering impressions in mind, at all times, according to the nature of their expression.

Take for example, the late *Sir Winston Churchill,* perhaps the outstanding personality of our time. What do you picture in mind when you think of him? A chubby-faced man with the eternal cigar, two fingers raised in a "V for Victory" salute, a square jaw creased by a grim smile—and you feel you are in the presence of the Rock of Gibraltar! How can you fail in your own life's battles when you reflect upon the spirit of leadership in such a man, in whom there was never any surrender? From individuals of Churchill's stature, we all draw strength to meet our own personal crises.

Mahatma Gandhi! At the mention of his name your mind conjures up the image of a frail, bent, dark-skinned little man, sitting cross-legged, attired in a loin cloth, smiling at you in almost toothless fashion. You marvel at the power he commanded by simple exercise of the mighty force of "peaceful resistance." You can still feel the spiritual nature of this man as you recall the dedicated manner in which he served his beloved people of India. And you realize that Gandhi has had his influence upon you—that your sympathetic, perhaps more understanding interest in the problems of his country was inspired by this truly great soul.

If you belong to the older generation and go back to the days of Will Rogers, you can picture America's world-famous cowboy humorist in your mind's eye, an unruly lock of brown hair down over his forehead, grinning, chewing gum and playing with a lasso, chuckling at his own jokes as he talks about all he knows—"what he reads in the newspapers." You can remember your sense of personal loss when you first heard the news of his death with Wiley Post in the airplane crash in the Arctic. You felt almost like a member of your own family had gone on. And you appreciate now that Will Rogers has left a part of his personality, his character, his spirit with you—that your life is that much richer because of his influence upon it.

Reflect upon the people, living and dead, who have never

caught the public eye but who have touched your life at some point, directly or indirectly, and whom you will never forget—who have impressed their personality upon you and who have had either a constructive or a destructive effect upon you.

Your father and mother, brothers or sisters, aunts and uncles, nieces and nephews, cousins, grandparents, in-laws, friends, business associates, neighbors, strangers—they all have played and are playing a part in your life.

You, as a personality in your own right, are surrounded by a host of personalities.

Are you standing out as an individual or are you over-shadowed, repressed, dominated or intimidated by stronger personalities?

Now that you have had this opportunity to size yourself up, how would you rate your personality as it is today? Are you at ease in any company, in command of any situation? Do you express yourself well and with assurance? Do you have a natural poise, a good posture and a positive bearing? Do you make an attractive appearance? Are you an entertaining conversationalist when the occasion demands? Do you know when it is wise to stop talking and to practice the art of listening? Are you informed on the events of the day, what's doing in sports, national and international affairs? Are you genuinely interested in others, their activities, their problems, even their different points of view?

This is all a part of personality expression, and you cannot successfully project your personality without it. If you find yourself lacking in any of these departments, concentrate on improvement in these areas.

"Take a gander" at yourself in the mirror. Study every physical movement. It tells a story. Each move you make marks your personality, in outer expression.

Examine that look on your face; it indicates the way you think. Your eyes—how do they appear to you? Are they clear, steady and direct? The person you see in the mirror is the one the other person sees. What kind of an impression do you wish to make on him? That's entirely up to you.

You know whether or not you are satisfied with your personality. If you are not, just wishing for it to change won't do it.

What is it, when you get in the presence of another person who has personality *plus*, that grips you? What is it that causes you to *feel* his very presence, that overshadows you, that compels attention and respect?

It's nothing more than a dynamic force, coupled with willpower, which he is drawing from that huge reservoir of the subconscious. There are millions of people who have this personality (some say it's natural with them, and perhaps it is, but they are unconsciously using this power). It has been thrust upon them, or they have developed it without realizing, early in life, and when that thing called personality is backed up with willpower and a desire to go places and do things, they get *action!*

The appealing personality belongs to that man or woman who possesses self-confidence, self-assurance. These are people with a purpose; they know where they are heading and how to get there, and this intensity of purpose shows in their faces. They have poise. They attract others to them like a giant magnet. Everyone just groups around a radiant personality.

When you get to know your real self, how you really feel and what you really desire in life, you can develop this same intensity of purpose, this determination to go, go, go! Once achieved, this determination will show in your eyes, your speech, your actions.

You have heard people say that a certain person has a penetrating gaze, that he looks right through one. What is it? Nothing more than that fire from within—intensity, or whatever you wish to call it—which means that the person who has that gaze usually gets what he wants. He compels, commands, attracts.

Remember, the eyes are the windows of the soul. Look at the photographs of successful men. Study their eyes and you will find that every one of them has that intensity. Therefore, I say, let it be reflected in the way you walk, in the way you carry yourself; soon people will begin to feel your presence when you pass through a crowd, take notice of you and want to know and listen to you.

AWAKEN! KNOW WHAT IS GOING ON ABOUT YOU! GET YOUR INTEREST UP IN PEOPLE AND EVENTS!

You can develop and expand your personality by keeping step with what is taking place in your community, your state, your country and the world's affairs. Keep informed. Find out all you can that is of interest about the people you have met and are to meet—you'll have much more in common to talk about. You never know what a new friend or prospect (if you are selling) may be interested in, and it's sometimes necessary to get his attention or your "big break," through entirely irrelevant subjects. You can't always start a conversation about the weather or your aches and pains. Read the newspapers, current periodicals, listen to important radio newscasts and television commentators. Use your eyes and ears. Be sure you're up-to-date. I don't mean to cover every detail of a murder or a suicide, but get a digest of the day's activities, at home and abroad. It will enlarge your perspective.

NEVER FORGET—KNOWLEDGE IS POWER! THAT MAY SOUND LIKE AN OLD BROMIDE, BUT, BROTHER, IT'S TRUE!

Who wants to listen to an uninformed, ignorant, self-centered individual?

166

Increase your knowledge, and the scope of your activities and interests will be greatly increased, as will the desire for greater things, larger things. As your desire expands, the things which you previously thought you wanted will seem to your mind to be trivial and you will disregard them, which is another way of saying that you ultimately will hitch your wagon to a star—and, when you do, you'll move with lightning-like speed!

Study, learn and work. Develop a keenness of observation. Step on the gas. Do better than that: get jet propulsion. Become alive for yourself, and you'll pass on this aliveness to the other fellow. You'll pep him up just by your being in his presence. Some of your magnetism will rub off on him, and he will like you for it. You've heard people say: "I get a big kick out of being with so-and-so. He (or she) always gives me a lift!"

Get confidence, enthusiasm, let loose some of that inner fire—"that something"—and you'll set up vibrations all around you. That's the theory of all life, as old as the world itself. *Like begets like*. A laugh brings a laugh; a good deed calls for a good deed; riches beget riches; love, love—you go on from there! It's contagious! The old law of attraction never fails!

But don't get the idea that I am giving you an oversized wishbone and all you have to do is sit down and start talking to yourself, and by using repetition, get what you want. It's not that easy! You've got to have the *wish*bone backed up with a *back*bone. And that isn't all. The *wish*bone and the *back*bone must be coordinated and synchronized to a point where they are operating in perfect harmony. When they are in tune, you will find personality developing. Then put action, energy into your scheme and everything will move before you.

I take it that all of us have admired that intense type of

person. I mean by that, one whose shoulders are back, whose chest is out, whose head is up and whose eyes are alert. It isn't hard to pick out in any organization those whose feet lag, whose shoulders droop, whose chins sag, and whose eyes are a blank. Drifters, loafers, quitters.

Are you close to that category? If you are, snap out of it!

> The fault, dear Brutus, is not in our stars,
> But in ourselves, that we are underlings.

William Shakespeare wrote that, as you know, and it's plain to be seen in his writings that he knew and used this inner power in his life. He rose high above the commonplace and won for himself an immortal niche in the literary · hall of fame, through reliance upon the creative power within.

Yes, the fault is in yourself, if you are not *what* you want to be, and *where* you want to be.

If you are timid, backward, in a rut and an underling, it is because of yourself. Blame not the stars. Blame not society. Blame not the world. Blame *yourself*. The time has come to change gears. Get out of low and shift into high. Start picturing what you really want to be, and you'll start to move.

Take warning that thought can operate in *reverse*. You can go backward through wrong thinking just as fast as you can go forward through right thinking.

This kind of "reverse thinking" has brought on depressions and can bring on depressions again. If the mind of man becomes panicky, if enough individuals become obsessed with fear and greed, if the psychology of scarcity sweeps through the land, if great numbers of people become too demanding or move too strongly in a certain direction, stock markets can become upset and the economy of the world can be affected.

You know, when you are depressed, you tend to depress

those around you. When the barometer falls it's a sign of storm conditions. A turned-down mouth has led to many turndowns. Don't carry your griefs and troubles around with you. No one wants to share them. People have griefs and troubles enough of their own.

Are you willing to put forth the effort to go higher than you have ever gone before? If you are, you are bound to greatly increase your *personal magnetism*. There was a time, remember, when the celebrities of yesterday and today were complete *unknowns*. Who are you to say you cannot be a great singer, an actor, an orchestra leader, a composer, an engineer, a scientist, a doctor, a business executive, a super salesman, an astronaut—whatever you desire—if you *work* at it and develop the personality, along with the skill, to get you there!

THOUGHTS TO BUILD INTO YOUR LIFE

My most valuable asset, insofar as my relations with others are concerned, is my personality and the manner in which I give expression to it.

I must make the best use of the body and mind with which I came into this world.

A study of the lives of successful men and women will give me the key to ways by which I may improve my own appearance and more dynamically express my personality.

I recognize that the fault lies largely in myself if I am not, as yet, what I want to be or where I want to be.

Adversities I have suffered or may encounter can develop in me greater strength of character and appeal of personality if I meet them constructively and seek to find a positive value in them.

It is my resolve to put forth every effort, each day, to increase my personal magnetism.

14

The Power of Influencing People

To be able to hold your own with others, personally, socially or in a business way, is a natural human desire.

You don't particularly enjoy being pushed aside or around, stepped on, walked over, and generally clobbered by unfeeling people who are only out for themselves and who would like to use you for a doormat, if you'd let them!

That's why, when you see courses and record albums advertised on "How to Make Others Do What You Want—Through Hypnotism (or Suggestion)," you quickly get your check in the mail! Or, when you receive a circular, advertising a book with the heading: *Men and Women Must Do Your Bidding—Learn How to Spot Their Hidden Weaknesses and Turn Them to Your Advantage,* you say, "That's for *me!* I'd like to be able to tell So-and-So where to go and what to do, for a change!"

Well, of course it's true that everyone has weaknesses. Even Achilles had a heel that was highly vulnerable. And there are times when you can take advantage of another's weakness and put something over on him. But instead of studying other people's weaknesses and trying to outsmart or outmaneuver them, you would be far better off trying to discover *your own weaknesses* and getting rid of them, so that you are protected against yourself!

This psychology of playing upon the weaknesses of others is a *negative* approach. All you need is an understanding of mind and emotions, and you will not only know how *you* think and feel, but you will also be able to sense and to judge the mental and emotional attitudes of *others*, and govern yourself accordingly in your associations and dealings with them.

It is far wiser to look for the good side in those whom you contact and to direct your appeal to that side, rather than to try to discern their weak points and seek to exploit them for your own advantage or gain.

There's no question about the tremendous power of suggestion. You've heard all your life how easy it is to make a person ill by constantly suggesting to him that he doesn't look well. If enough people conspire to do this, the average individual can't take it. He actually gets sick.

Now, if you encountered a person who was highly suggestive, you could conceivably go to work on him and cause him to do things really against his will. He could well resent this later and hate you for it. A salesman, operating on a one-time, once-around basis, and not caring what a prospect thinks of him—just out to make a sale and get going—might employ this kind of selling tactics. If he does so, he makes it plenty rough on the next salesman. He is sowing seeds of distrust, lack of confidence and ill-feeling, which will catch up with him in time, like the boomerang that always comes back to the thrower.

There is an art in influencing people, in getting them to make up their minds, to see your point of view, to go along with you on a community project, or a personal matter or a business deal, or to buy something you are selling or to accept you as a friend or a sweetheart.

THE APPEAL TO SELF-INTEREST

Most effective of all approaches to any person, at any time, is your appeal to his self-interest. When you demonstrate a sincere interest in the activities or ambitions or problems of any man or woman or child, you can command their attention as well as their appreciation. Find and concentrate upon the outstanding self-interest of any individual and you have an increasing influence over him or her. Since "like always attracts like," remember: a genuine display of interest in someone, expressed in word and deed, begets an interest in *you* in return.

In true selling, and in true human relationships, something of equal value must be exchanged between the seller and the buyer. Each must feel he is benefiting from the transaction. It's as simple and basic as this. To have a friend, you must be a friend. To make a sale, you must inspire good feeling and confidence.

The power of influencing people is a power that can be misused and abused. You should never attempt to sell anything in which you do not honestly believe. You may be able to do it by turning on the charm of your personality, by whipping up a pretense of enthusiasm, by pressure tactics and by deceitful or exaggerated statements and promises. But if you are conscientious and have retained any genuine feeling of ethics, you will secretly hate yourself, while raking in the money.

Some salesmen I have known have excused their selling techniques by saying: "If I didn't sell these suckers, someone else would do it, the same way. As a matter of fact, that's the system my competitor is using and if I don't beat the bushes just as hard, I won't get my share of the business."

This kind of selling often leaves a wreckage of disillusioned and disgruntled buyers in its wake. It is also the road to ulcers and other bodily ills contracted by mentally and emotionally disturbed salesmen. They require constant buildups in the form of "pep sessions" and booster talks, to send them out on the "firing line" each day. Eventually, those who are not sufficiently calloused or "conditioned" find it impossible to continue "forced selling" methods on services and products that they know do not possess the values claimed for them; they begin to experience a kickback in the stomach and solar plexus regions, as well as congested feelings in the nerve centers in the backs of their necks.

Nor can they keep up this day-by-day high-pressure business without bringing about personality changes, most damaging of which will be their gradual loss of self-respect, honesty and sincerity. After awhile, as they go on making false statements and assurances to maintain pre-set sales goals, they won't even be believing in themselves! In due course of time, they will commence to unconsciously radiate a "phony atmosphere," and while their personalities may be expansive enough to keep on attracting new prospects, what they have *become* will be sensed by discerning people who will no longer accept what they say as truthful or dependable.

"I used to like So-and-So," a friend said to me, in referring to a man we both knew. "There was a time when he could sell me anything. Now, I try to duck when I see him coming because I know he is going to work on me, pulling out all the emotional stops and giving me the old, manufactured sales pitch, which he doesn't really mean and doesn't believe himself!"

I agreed that this man had lost much of his former appeal and the confidence he had at one time inspired. Then my friend went on: "I wish he'd get back to the simple, sincere guy he used to be, and line up with a reputable sales organization—but he says there's not enough money in these standard items, and he can make a lot more on the stuff he is selling. In my book, he's a good salesman gone wrong!"

The essence of selling is to sell yourself first, making it a point to establish faith and confidence of the prospect in you. This cannot be done unless you yourself possess character and integrity. When I say "it cannot be done," I mean it cannot be done *safely* and *successfully*. However, a clever "con" man, who knows the psychology of selling, how to use the power of suggestion and how to exploit the self-interest of people, can still get them to buy the Brooklyn Bridge or a set of false teeth for a toothless housecat. But he is compelled to keep on the move. He doesn't dare return to the same sales territory. His mesmerizing influence over those he has sold is always short-lived.

WE HAVE ALL BEEN "TAKEN"

You and I each have an area of vulnerability. No matter how much we may know about human psychology or how prepared we think we may be against the mental manipulations of designing men and women who are out to "feather their own nests" at our expense, we must constantly be on guard to keep, on occasion, from "being taken."

I knew better, but a few years ago I permitted a charming and persuasive younger man to sell me a bill of goods that cost me heavily in time and money and contributed to a physical illness.

How did he do it? By appealing to my *self-interest*. For years I had dreamed of being a part, one day, of a foundation dedicated to research in the field of extrasensory perception. I had hoped to aid in securing large sums of money to make possible the employment of top scientists and laboratory facilities, as well as outstanding "sensitives" (men and women possessing demonstrated telepathic and other extrasensory powers) so that knowledge of these mysterious higher faculties of mind might be vastly increased during my lifetime.

This younger man, whom we will call Mr. "X," had been highly successful in California real estate. He was rated as being worth some six to seven million dollars, according to Dun & Bradstreet. He had just finished building some thirty beautiful homes, to sell for fifty to a hundred thousand dollars each, atop a prominence overlooking the Pacific Ocean.

"I have always been interested in ESP," he said, "since attending your lectures and reading your books some years ago. It opened my eyes to the possibilities of mental development, and now that I am in the money, I would like to make a million dollars available for research. Do you suppose you could line up some of the top scientists and people in this ESP field and interest them in establishing a foundation which would be international in scope, aligning itself with the reputable research being undertaken by scientists in various parts of the world?"

Mr. "X" was saying exactly what I had longed to hear someone, who had the means to back it up, say. I promised to try to see what I could do, and we had long and what appeared to be enthusiastic discussions relative to the setting up of such a foundation. Certainly *I* was enthused, because Mr. "X" was expressing an interest in financing record albums that I had prepared (based on different self-help books of mine) and in working out methods of distribution and so on. In moments of reflection, it seemed almost "too good to be true," but I did not call upon my "intuition" to guide me, to get a sensing of just how genuine this entire proposition might be. Looking back, I guess I just wanted this to be true since I had dreamed of such a project for so long. I didn't want the dream to be shattered. And so, I brought this Mr. "X" in touch with top people; some of them were flown in for consultation. He met influential friends of mine in the California area. Each and all of them were favorably impressed, which naturally bolstered my confidence.

As plans progressed, Mr. "X" offered to set aside for occupancy by top scientists five of his most beautiful, newly completed homes that commanded a magnificent view of the expanse of the Pacific and mountain areas in and around.

"One of these homes is to be for you and Mrs. Sherman," he said, as he showed them to us. "I will have one for my wife and family. One will be held as a residence for guest scientists visiting the foundation from different parts of the world. The other two are for the scientists who have agreed to join us and will be active in foundation work."

How could any arrangement be more ideal, on the surface? Mrs. Sherman and I protested that we were not accustomed to this kind of luxurious living, that we had been apartment-house dwellers most of our lives, in New York, Chicago and Los Angeles, that we traveled much in lecturing, and that our permanent home had been established and would always remain in the Ozarks, in north-central Arkansas.

"That's perfectly all right," said Mr. "X," "You will be able to return to your Arkansas home a number of months each year, but you will always have this house to return to as executive director of this foundation. I feel it is imperative that this foundation, if it is to be represented by the top people in the extrasensory field, must look the part, to properly impress the public."

Since I am not, and never will be a business man, why should I argue against such arrangements? They seemed acceptable to all concerned, and Mr. "X" said he had ordered his attorneys to draw up plans for incorporating the foundation. He then took us by car to a location, also overlooking the ocean, which he proposed as the site for the foundation buildings and laboratories.

"I own these twenty acres," he said, "and they are not far from big private military installations. This is going to be a 'Think Center' for the top scientists and engineers in the country, and we will have access to the services of many of them because I am already in touch with Government and military heads of some of their building projects."

Approaching the "dawn"!

Came the day when offices were set up in a new office building near the coast, and Mrs. Sherman and I left our Hollywood apartment to take an apartment in the area so that we would be spared the long drive each day to and from the office address. The "new home" was not yet ready for occupancy although a "Sold" sign had been put up on the lawns of all five of the homes which were to be reserved for the foundation.

"We are having a little difficulty with the County over roads and installations, which is preventing us, temporarily, from opening these properties and homes for sale," Mr. "X" explained.

A part of the office space was set aside for Mr. "X" and his real-estate operations. He told us this would permit him to divide his time between his other business enterprises and the work which the ESP foundation was to conduct, as well as to give attention to the promotion of my self-development record albums.

There was much coming and going of people obviously not related to my projects, and Mr. "X" was seen less and less. Since I was supposed to consult with him before taking action, there was little or nothing for me to do, and now, at last, I began to wonder. Mrs. Sherman and I had been willing to change drastically our own way of living, and I

178

had given up a number of lucrative writing assignments to be of assistance in setting up the foundation so that some top scientists could take over in the research end. Mr. "X" had offered me a beginning salary, saying that when the time came for him to contribute the million dollars to the foundation, it would assume the responsibility of paying for the services of those actively engaged. But within two weeks the beginning salary was cut in half, and Mr. "X" indicated it would take him longer than he had anticipated to liquidate some of his holdings and to get the foundation legally and officially under way.

The day of disillusionment

One day a man introduced himself to me, identifying himself as one of Mr. "X's" real-estate associates. He said he thought there were a few things I ought to know.

Number One: Mr. "X" was in financial difficulties. He had been under pressure the past ninety days from loan companies that had financed his building operations. He had held them off from closing in on him by telling them that he was about to set up a big ESP foundation with top names, and that the money that would be subscribed for this foundation would be invested in this real-estate project, enabling him to launch a promotion that would put everyone financially in the clear.

Number Two: One of the wealthy people to whom I had introduced Mr. "X," and on whom the latter had counted to match the million dollars worth of assets he, "X", was to put into the foundation, had refused to go along until and unless Mr. "X" put his money up first.

Number Three: Mr. "X" was so involved that he could not put up any money at present; his entire time and efforts would have to be devoted to getting out from under, since he could not hold off the loan companies and other creditors any longer.

179

This was obviously news I did not want to hear. No one likes to have a dream shattered into which he has put all his hopes and aspirations, and, if you like, his life's blood.

When I confronted Mr. "X," he dismissed the matter with little more than a wave of his hand. Yes, he unfortunately could not go through with either the foundation plan or the promotion of my records at this time. But he was glad that he had at least been able to get me started, and that I was welcome to continue in these offices, taking over the rental and other costs, if I could get the financing. He would help later, as soon as he could get certain things straightened out.

This was the last I ever saw of Mr. "X" personally, except at a distance. He moved in and out of his offices, passing me as though I did not exist. There was nothing hostile; I had just been dismissed; whatever usefulness I might have been to him was at an end. I packed up my personal belongings and took my leave of the beautiful new office space and the headquarters of the foundation that was not to be. Of course I was deeply embarrassed to have brought top people into this situation with me, but profoundly grateful that neither they nor I had proceeded to the point where any of us could be seriously hurt. I was left temporarily with a helpless, deeply hurt feeling that promptly materialized into a *severe attack of sciatica*. I will have more to say about this phase of the experience in the chapter on "Healing."

Picking up the pieces, leaving the area, returning to an apartment in Hollywood near our former address and resuming activities in my own field of creative writing and lecturing was not an easy adjustment, but it was accomplished.

MY OWN SELF TO BLAME

Why have I disclosed to you, in detail, this most disillusioning of all my life experiences? Because so many of you have been "taken" on various propositions of this nature. My files contain scores of letters recounting how husbands and wives had trustingly invested their life savings on "get-rich-quick schemes" or "humanitarian projects" that were going to "do humanity much good" but that only contributed to the welfare of those who fleeced them.

No doubt you have been duped at least once in your life. You have permitted yourself to be "influenced" by a "con" man or woman who said just the things you wanted to hear, made just the right representations and gave you just the right "window dressing" to impress you and cause you to become disastrously involved.

So many have asked me how they could recover their money from such operators? Some have gone into costly court cases. Others have tried all manner of personal appeals and threats. In most instances, however, their money is not recoverable and they might better free their minds of the worry over the loss and resolve to avoid succumbing to any such *influences* in the future.

As for myself, I have long since refused to carry hate and resentment toward anyone who has done me harm in any way. I can truthfully say that I hold no ill will toward Mr. "X." I even find myself wondering at times if, regardless of the economic jam he was in, he didn't sincerely believe he could put over this "grandiose scheme," thus "killing two birds with one stone," helping himself and helping me set up this foundation, which could have been a fine development, once realized. This is certainly giving him the benefit of every doubt and may be too kind a consideration. Strangely enough, many of the people who are engaged in promoting offbeat projects possess disarmingly appealing personalities. If not sincere, they hypnotize themselves into believing that they have a good purpose behind their machinations. They are past masters at sensing what you want and putting that *want* into words, with such apparent sincerity and conviction that it would require the exercise of *extrasensory perception* to detect their *real* motivations!

So—tell yourself now you will go slow when anyone approaches you with a proposition that seems "too good to be true." Once you allow yourself to be brought under the "influence" of the persuasive powers of any person, your mind is so responsive to suggestion that you may capitulate.

In my case, I had checked with friends upon whose judgment I depended, and they, too, had been taken in. But, fundamentally, I blame myself. I let my "self-interest" carry me away. And what has this experience taught me? That you should rarely, if ever, put your eggs in another person's basket, because all your eggs are apt to be broken.

Today, I am president and executive director of my own foundation—by name, ESP Research Associates Foundation, with offices in 1750 Tower Building, Little Rock, Arkansas. While it is not endowed with a million-dollar backing, it is free of any entanglements and will, in time, I believe, be able to enter the field of research in a way that will enable my long-standing dream to be realized. The California experience taught me how *not* to bring my dream into existence, proof again that you can profit by all past experiences, however costly, if you do not lose faith in yourself and your fellow man.

USE OF SUGGESTION IN INFLUENCING PEOPLE

Suggestion is one of the most powerful forces in the world. It has equal power in two directions—positive and negative—dependent on which direction you give it.

Those of you who are salesmen or who have your own business can testify to the power of suggestion. If, when others tell you that business is bad, things are tough, going to the bowwows and so on, you accept their negative thoughts and make them your own, your business *will* go to the bowwows. Have no doubt about that. Then, as you talk to others, with your chin on your chest, your feet dragging and the attitude of a professional mourner, passing on your pessimistic feelings, they become inoculated, and things continue to get worse, for you, and for them.

You are setting up thought, in reality *fear* thought, vibrations, which are far reaching. Fear thoughts are terribly contagious and spread like wildfire. Conversely, as you refuse to be influenced by the apprehensive predictions and lamentations of others and persist in picturing the improvement of your business, your sales, your profits, having no misgivings of your own, your business, your sales and your profits will automatically increase!

You must keep in mind always that the intense fire of genuine enthusiasm from within becomes a conflagration that affects all on your wavelength as long as you radiate it. The vibrations you set up with your powerful rays of enthusiasm inspire others, raise them up to your level, build and attract business—just as fear vibrations start downward spirals and lead to depression and failure.

When you need "building up," you can use suggestion upon yourself to excellent advantage. Now that you know the potency of thought, every time you catch yourself taking on negative mental attitudes about anything you are doing, or concerning your future—*stop everything!* Recognize at once the damage you are doing to yourself by permitting such thoughts to reside in your consciousness. Replace these wrong mental pictures immediately with strong visual suggestions of the right kind. *See yourself* overcoming whatever difficulties you are facing, doing a better job, getting a better result tomorrow.

Remember, I repeat again: the creative power within can only work on what you give it! A builder has to operate from a blueprint. If there are defects in the blueprint, and he doesn't know about them, those defects will show up in the completed building. Unless you discover your wrong thinking the wrong suggestions you are giving yourself each day—you'll attract what you are visualizing to you. Pass those suggestions on to your friends or associates and, if they accept them, they'll help you produce the very conditions you have pictured!

THE SUGGESTIVE POWER OF HYPNOTISM

Experiments in hypnotism have demonstrated in many ways the power of suggestion. Once the resistance of the conscious mind has been removed, so that the subconscious mind can be reached directly, the latter will respond instantly to whatever suggestions are given it, if what is suggested is within the moral standards of the individual. When suggestions repugnant to the basic character of the person are made, he either refuses to respond or comes out from under the hypnotic spell. It would require a series of suggestions designed to alter the present moral concepts before the individual would be willing to perform any act against his fixed standard of conduct. This clearly indicates that you do not change your acts until you change your mind; what you have become through past experience and thought you remain, until something brings about a change in your own thinking.

YOU CAN BE INFLUENCED WHILE YOU SLEEP

Psychologists and psychiatrists are finding that many people can be helped to overcome various faults and personal habits, inhibitions and inferiorities if suggestions are made at their bedsides while they sleep. The subconscious mind never sleeps. It is always aware of what is going on, in and about you. Often, however, when you are mentally and emotionally disturbed and wish to control your mind and your feelings you find it almost impossible to do so during your waking hours. If a loved one, with whom you have a sympathetic, understanding bond, could softly but positively suggest, after you have dropped off to sleep, that you will overcome your difficulties, these thoughts might lodge in your consciousness and aid you in developing a more positive attitude. This should only be done during the "twilight zone of sleep." Deep sleep suggestions are *seldom effective*.

All life is really suggestion. You are constantly accepting or rejecting each experience that comes to you. If you accept it, your mind is acting upon it, for good or ill, dependent on the nature and character of the experience.

WHAT ARE WE DOING TO THE CHILD MIND?

Speaking of influencing people, what are we doing to the minds of our children? Aren't we, as parents and elders, constantly bombarding youngsters with destructive suggestions:

"Don't go out dressed that way—you'll catch your death of cold!"

"Look out—you'll get run over!"

"Don't touch that—you'll break it!"

"I knew you'd do that! Can't you watch what you're doing?"

"Don't stay out late—something may happen to you!"

"Stay away from the water—you might get drowned!"

"You can't do that—better let me do it for you!"

"For heaven's sake, keep quiet! You don't know anything!"

"No, of course not—I don't trust you!"

"If you don't stop that, I'll call a policeman and have you locked up!"

"You shouldn't ask questions like that—you're not old enough to know the answers!"

185

"So, you've done it again! Well, that's just what I expected!"

"Go away, you're a nuisance! I don't know why you were ever born!"

"Why, you little brat! I'm so mad I could kill you!"

You've heard these delightful suggestions and many, many more. The only wonder is that children, subjected to this kind of highly emotionalized, wrong thinking, turn out as well as they do!

No doubt many parents are driven to distraction and beyond by the antics of their offspring, and feel called upon to use anything short of mayhem to get the children to mind them, but it is unwise to resort to fearsome and destructive suggestions as corrective measures. When a child is thus reprimanded, especially if he is in an emotional state, these wrong mental pictures of mishaps and misconduct and your own emphasizing of his defects take hold of his consciousness, causing him to develop a greater susceptibility toward the very things you want him to avoid or eliminate.

The homely or awkward or backward child starts out with natural handicaps, anyway, and if parents or elders constantly remind the child (repetition, reiteration) how homely or awkward he is, the child tends to become even more so. These are the very children who are in need of the finest kind of positive suggestions. Some teachers are now recognizing this need and are saying privately to unattractive or backward children, as they get the opportunity, "You're getting better looking every day! . . . You're doing much better!" Like little plants that have been lacking in nourishment, these children respond and unfold remarkably in a short time. Try this method; reinforce it with the expression of *love*—and watch miracles happen!

What you do and what you say, how you express your personality in the presence of others, is having a suggestive

186

effect upon them, and as I have said, they, in turn are having a suggestive effect upon you.

If others criticize you or don't believe you are capable of doing what you want to do don't accept their suggestions! Analyze yourself to determine whether or not their criticism is justified; if it is, remove any resentment you may feel because of this criticism, give thanks that these defects were called to your attention and get busy eliminating them so that they will no longer hinder your upward progress. But maintain belief in yourself. If you lose this, you lose everything! All success, big or small, starts with faith in self and faith in the creative power within. You must have it, you must retain it, to go from where you are to where you want to be!

INFLUENCING YOURSELF TO MAKE MONEY!

Perhaps one of your biggest problems in life is making money. If it is, you should learn how to use the power of your TNT to *get* money.

Some people are so accustomed to being without money that they can't picture anything else. They are like the poor down-and-outer who was asked: "Sam, if you had five dollars in your pocket, what would you do?" Instantly came the rueful answer: "I'd wonder *whose* pants I had on!"

Have you fallen into the mental rut of *picturing* yourself with a flat bank account and a flat pocketbook? If you have, you have been creating near poverty instead of prosperity.

If you continue to tell yourself that you aren't worth much, that you will never be worth any more, that you don't know where your next dollar's coming from, you are actually telling your creative power within—your TNT —that there is nothing it can do to help you, that you are next door to the poorhouse and there is no way out!

Is this what you want? Of course not! But you will get something like this if you *keep on picturing* it!

Nor will God step in to help you, because God has given you *unlimited* power within to call upon in time of need—the God-given power to attract all the opportunities and resources necessary, IF you will only direct this power—command it to do your bidding—by giving it the right mental pictures of what you desire.

I have to repeat and repeat and repeat this GREAT fact because it is so vitally important to your success and prosperity!

You will have the right influence upon other people if you exercise the right influence over yourself. Give yourself these suggestions every night, during a quiet moment, before retirement:

"Each day I am going to improve and eventually I will remove the faults I discover in myself. Each day I am going to attain greater control of my mind and emotions. Each day I am going to overcome more of my fears and worries and other destructive thoughts. Each day I am developing greater health, happiness and prosperity. Each day I am going to find finer opportunities for serving others and doing worthwhile things. Each day I am going to make the right impression on others so they will want to do things for and with me. *Each day....*"

You take it up from here. Create your own tomorrows by your own *positive suggestions* as applied to yourself and your needs.

THOUGHTS TO BUILD INTO YOUR LIFE

The power to influence people is a power that can be misused and abused.

It is wrong to attempt to influence a person against his will. This will always lead to a destructive kick-back, in time.

Self-interest is the most powerful interest there is—and when I am appealing to another's self-interest, I am most apt to sell or influence him in my favor.

Regardless of what has been done to me by others who have influenced me to engage in costly ventures of time and money, I refuse to carry hate or resentment toward them.

I will assume my share of the responsibility for any unhappy adventures and involvements, in the faith that, detached and demagnetized from wrong or undesirable people, I can move on, with a free mind, to better things.

I will always keep in mind that what I do and say, how I express myself in the presence of others, is having a suggestive effect upon them, and that they, in turn, are having a suggestive effect upon me.

I declare, here and now, that I will not accept any negative suggestions from others and that I will not permit my own mind to create anything but positive suggestions as applied to me.

Each day I am resolved to remove the faults I discover in myself—to make the right impression on others so they will want to do things for and with me.

Each day I am going to look for finer opportunities to serve others and to do worthwhile things!

15

The Power of Getting Along With Others

There is one new cabinet post that should be established in our Federal Government. For that matter, this kind of office should be set up as a vital branch of any nation's administration.

It is—*The Secretary of HUMAN RELATIONS!* This department would become, at once, the busiest in the land. Its primary aim would be to help individuals get along with one another. This inability to live always peacefully under the same roof, with next-door neighbors, with in-laws, with fellow workers, with business associates, with club members, with schoolmates, with church people, with political opponents, with anyone and everyone, is a plague upon men and women, young and old, everywhere!

The threat of a third World War starts with two individuals who can't get along, multiplied by millions whose hates and resentments and fears and suspicions are keeping them from getting along with the peoples of other countries. The mass consciousness of mankind is in a highly emotional, disturbed state at present and is apt to remain so for some time. You can do little about this, but you can do a great deal toward attaining and maintaining your own peace of mind, and establishing good human relations with loved ones, friends and all whom you will meet.

JEALOUSY—LEADING CAUSE OF POOR RELATIONS

Jealousy can be ruinous to human happiness. And yet we are all guilty of it at times.

It is often difficult for you to see some individual get credit for something which you feel should have come to *you*.

Or perhaps a business associate or fellow worker gets a promotion when you do not, making you jealous or resentful.

A brother or sister or some other relative may be favored by those you love and may enjoy a greater popularity. This is almost certain cause for a jealous reaction.

So-and-So may have more money, more advantages in life —all the things you'd like to have and can't afford, so you "burn up" every time you think of what he or she has, and what you *haven't*.

It isn't fair. It isn't right. This life is all wrong.

Yes, I concede that this life is full of injustices, inequities, unfortunate occurrences. But if you and I are to derive any lasting degree of happiness from it, we must adjust ourselves to the daily happenings so that we are not emotionally upset each time we encounter an unpleasant human experience.

Why let yourself be made miserable by the actions of others?

You can, if you will, school yourself not to "fly off the handle" when others mistreat you—and even to return kindness for offense and insult.

If another individual is jealous of you, he may try to hurt your feelings or embarrass you, and he would like nothing better than to see that you are affected by what he does or says. Unless you maintain good emotional control, you will give such a person great satisfaction. But if you overlook the intended slight, you will do more to punish a jealous friend or relative than to give recognition to his thoughts and acts. A bitter attack upon a jealous individual will only further aggravate matters and create a breach between the two of you that can never again be closed in friendship.

Jealousy is a terrible, vicious, destructive emotion. Not so long ago, a woman dropped a note out of an apartment window, saying she was being held prisoner by her husband —and pleading for someone to rescue her. Police called at the address, found an attractive woman, locked in a room where she had been kept by a jealous husband who resented other men looking at her when they were out together. Of course, her husband was emotionally unbalanced but there are thousands of other men and women who are motivated by jealousy to say and do mean things to their mates.

Some women make the great mistake of "playing a romantic game" with their husbands. The idea is to keep them guessing as to whether or not they really still love them. This is supposed to keep their mates "pursuing them," after the "chase" has been ended by marriage. These women are afraid that romance will become commonplace unless they are wooed every day by their men—"wooed all over again."

Obviously, the love of no man or woman should be taken for granted. Romantic attentions should not cease with the ringing of wedding bells. Playing, however, with a man's or a woman's affections, after marriage, is dynamite. Then is the time to give your mate daily assurance of your love for him or her—to leave no room for doubt or jealousy or discord.

If you find you are jealous of someone—ask yourself— WHY? Is it because you really feel inferior to this person, incapable of being what he or she has become? If so—put your jealousy aside and go to work on yourself. You have a reconstruction job to do, with respect to your personality, character and ability. When this has been accomplished, you will have attained recognition on your own merits, and developed beyond the temptation to envy others.

You can well afford to be generous in your estimate of others, whatever their estimate of you. This does not mean that you have to go over-board or to be extravagant in any expressed praise or appreciation. Sometimes what you do not say is safer and wiser than saying anything. But jealousy, under any and all circumstances, is not a power—it is a weakness! You cannot think clearly and correctly while dominated by it.

HYPERSENSITIVITY CAN CAUSE TROUBLE

Are you hypersensitive? Do you imagine that you aren't making the proper impression on people, that you haven't said or done the right thing? Do you keep going over and over what you have said and done, afterward, wishing you had said or done something else and fearing you have offended friends or that they have misunderstood your actions?

This is a bad mental habit, usually caused by an over-conscientious attitude. You quite possibly were criticized in your childhood for things you said and did that disturbed your elders, and you have feared, ever since, that your conduct might not be acceptable to others.

"I am always imagining that my remarks may be misinterpreted by friends," an influential businessman confessed to me. "I catch myself apologizing for fancied slights of others, only to find that my friends don't know what I'm apologizing about. This apprehension that whatever I do or say may be wrong is making me nervous and affecting my health."

A prominent society woman said to me: "Everyone thinks it is easy for me to appear in public and take part in social functions. Actually it is torture because I live in fear that I will make a fool of myself. I never do, of course, but it's an ordeal for me to face people and to take charge of meetings. I'm never sure how I've made out until it's all over. In fact,

I think I'm making a botch of things at the time. I'd give anything if I could get rid of these inferior feelings."

The cure for hypersensitivity is in realizing that there is no justification for your fears. You have not made the wrong impression on others, despite your worries. Your failure has been in your mind only. But continued worry of this kind, unless checked, can eventually demoralize you and upset your powers of expression to the point that you will not be able to think and act as you should.

Some men and women have taken to drink to give them greater assurance, to blind them to certain mistakes they may make and to give them "courage" to speak out and do as they like. Using alcohol as a prop seemingly aids some people in the meeting of others, but their sense of inferiority will get them into trouble, sooner or later. You cannot eliminate *hypersensitivity* with liquor or any other bad fault.

Give thought in advance to the people you are apt to meet at a coming social function. Picture yourself meeting them in a relaxed, self-confident way. See yourself showing an interest in these people, asking them about their activities, talking about subjects of interest to them. When you keep your mind's attention upon others, you cannot be worrying about what others are thinking about you, and you will naturally say and do the right thing as you react to what is being said and done by others.

Only when you are self-consciously aware of every move you make in the presence of others, are you plagued with these apprehensions that you aren't doing so well. Forget yourself, and you will be remembered favorably by those you meet.

ANOTHER WAY NOT TO GET ALONG WITH OTHERS

Do you "kill" your friends and loved ones with kindness? Do you insist on doing things for others whether or not they want you to do them or *prefer* to do these things for themselves?

This is a mistaken way of demonstrating your affection for friends and loved ones. There is a joy in doing, from which others should not be deprived.

You may get a big kick out of serving your friends and loved ones when such services really aren't welcome.

"I let So-and-So do things for me because she insists on doing them," a friend said to me, "but I wish to goodness, she *wouldn't!* She makes me feel eternally under obligation to her but, worst of all, she does things that I'd prefer doing for myself!"

Such "serving of others" is really a form of selfishness or "smother love." You aren't doing these things to bring others happiness as much as yourself.

Some mothers and fathers pour out this kind of devotion upon their children, trying to participate as much as possible in their lives—to the extent that the children are semi-helpless to do anything for themselves, even their own thinking. Then such parents, when their children act rebellious or get into an escapade, often say: "That's gratitude after all I've done for you, the sacrifices I've made—no appreciation. I can't understand your turning out like you have!"

Taking away an individual's self-reliance, the incentive to do things for one's self, can develop in such a person life-lasting inferiorities.

Self-sufficient grown-ups will resent your attempt to do things that they prefer doing for themselves. They may put up with your "devotion" for a time, but you will be destroying rather than increasing their affection by hovering over and around them, endeavoring to anticipate their every need and jumping in, unasked, to "be helpful."

The best rule is to be ready and willing to do things for those you love, but to make sure that such services are welcome and invited before insisting or volunteering to render them.

Take pride in the accomplishments of friends and relatives, encourage them to do things for themselves; in this way, you will not only help create more capable individuals, but you will also give them a true joy in their own attainments.

A little boy pathetically said, when he had ridden a few feet on a bicycle without his parent's guiding hands: "Did *I* do it—or *didn't* I?" His face glowed when he was assured that he had done it, all by himself.

One of the strongest human desires of young or old is to be able to "do" things. It is a danger signal when you want to give up and let others do things for you that you could really do for yourself. Of course, if health or other factors will not permit, this is different. But don't let others "kill you with kindness," and don't *you* try to "kill" them.

"*Live and let live*" is a policy that will bring you more friends and influence people to love you.

FEAR OF WHAT OTHERS MAY THINK

Are you afraid of what others may think? Do you let this fear keep you from doing and saying things that should be done and said?

Many men and women of good moral character are permitting fear of ridicule, criticism or censure to destroy their much greater usefulness to the community in which they live. They are afraid to take a stand on any controversial issue that may come up for fear of offending friends who may oppose it.

"I'm going to stay out of this," such persons will say. "You don't need my vote or opinion or help, anyway. I can't afford to antagonize So-and-So—he's too good a friend or customer of mine."

But if Mr. So-and-So is not acting for the best interests of the community, he *should* be opposed, and you are not a good citizen if you fail to take a public stand for community betterment.

Fear of gossip has kept numerous men and women from talking or associating with neighbors whose reputation has been sullied by those who have not approved of their actions. They are afraid to be seen with certain persons on the street lest the "scandal brigade" start their "tongues wagging."

Ask yourself only one question if and when you are confronted with the same fear of "what others may say":

> *Knowing that we all have our faults, is there anything really wrong in my talking or associating with So-and-So, just so I know my own conduct, regardless of what others may think or say, is beyond reproach?*

If the answer you get from your own conscience clears you of any malicious comments that may be made, feel free to think and act as you choose.

Who is running your life, anyway—you or the small-minded citizens of your community?

DO "THINGS" POSSESS YOU?

You love your home, of course, or—at least—you *should.* There is something very wrong if you don't, but have you ever considered what makes a happy home? The answer is simple—the *people* in it! Not the *things*—the *people!*

You hear folks say: "So-and-So has a wonderful home!"

Does he? He may have a beautiful home and yard, a two-car garage, every modern convenience and gadget—and yet the life in his home may be far from happy.

We spend far too much emotion and sentiment upon *things* and possessions which really possess US, rather than our possessing them. And because *things* have come to mean more to many men and women than they themselves do to each other, true happiness has vanished from their lives. In its place is a synthetic kind of happiness such as the cheap joy which selfish ownership brings.

"She just lives for her home," one woman said of another, and she spoke the truth.

This woman was living for her house rather than her husband and family. She loved every piece of antique furniture in it; she kept everything in order as one would a showcase or a set of museum pieces. You mustn't sit in this chair or that chair—they were too valuable and your weight might break them. Make certain your shoes aren't muddy before walking upon her costly carpetings. The personal value she attached to her furnishings destroyed their utility. They were to be admired but used with such great care that other members of the household found no happiness living in such an atmosphere, especially the children, who rebelled against the restrictions of "Don't touch this and that." This was an extreme case, but there are many lesser cases of foolish and unwarranted devotion to *things*—to the extent that things have come between the love of a man and wife for each other.

Things can be clothes as well as a house or furniture, and an inordinate desire to put everything on one's back is another form of selfishness that arouses resentment.

Things can also include an excessive interest in a dog—devoting more attention to it than one's mate. Or *things* can mean an interest in horse racing or gambling or away-from-home activities that take too much time and money and tend to destroy the home life of the individual.

Are you a worshipper of THINGS? It's fine to have nice things if nice things don't have YOU! Love of home and family puts things, which possess no happiness in and of themselves, in their rightful place.

Without the PEOPLE in a home and their devotion to one another there is no happiness worthy of the name and there never will be.

SHOWING INTEREST AND APPRECIATION BEST WAY TO GET ALONG WITH OTHERS

What is the most appreciated compliment you can p y to a friend or loved one?

Giving considerate and devoted attention to that man or woman's interests, activities, desires and aspirations!

If you are thoughtless, indifferent or disinterested in the presence of a friend, sweetheart, wife or husband, you can, in time, lose that individual's regard and respect for you.

"He used to shower me with every courtesy and attention," a young, disillusioned married woman said to me, recently. "But now he just takes me for granted. When we go places, he acts as though he hardly knows I'm along—or cares. He has his eyes for other young women and centers his attentions on them, turning his charm and his entertaining qualities in their direction. Then, when the time comes to go home, he suddenly remembers I'm around somewhere and picks me up, telling me what a wonderful time 'we've' had!"

Yes, there are plenty of men and women like this, BUT quite often the mate so treated is partly to blame. In this case, the young married woman admitted that she didn't get a big bang out of her husband's witticisms and attempts to be the life of the party. This being true, he naturally satisfied his urge for social expression on those who gave him an appreciative audience—and let his wife sit it out. Had she shown him that she liked his attentions, that they meant as much to her as they had in the days of their courtship, the chances are he would have tried standing on his head in the parlor—if he knew this would please her.

We all like to "star in someone's life," to be the focal point of attention, to know that someone loves us and cares about what happens to us, how we feel, what we do and think. If our mate loses interest, most of us seek understanding companionship elsewhere.

A self-centered man or woman can drive a mate to drink. He or she may not realize what this interest in self is doing to a life partner. You've met the type:

"Oh, darling, I've had a perfectly miserable day today. The washing machine broke . . . and Mary ruined that new dress climbing a fence . . . and I had a run-in with our landlady . . . and . . ."

Everything happens to such an individual who dramatizes these events. Perhaps the husband has had a rough day at the office and tries to communicate this fact:

"That's tough, dear, but wait till you hear what's happened to *me*. . . !"

This is as far as he gets. She's not interested in *his* story, and she hasn't half finished with *hers*. Each day is just a succession of unhappy episodes involving herself. She has no time or desire to learn about and to sympathize with what her husband has encountered. It's "me—me—me" all the time until he can't take it any more and ends up at a bar or tavern, pouring out his own hard luck to some equally dissatisfied man or woman who, like himself, is seeking an understanding listener.

Attention, personal attention, is a deep craving of the human soul. But we mustn't drive our loved ones away by demanding complete attention and not giving any. There is a time to listen and a time to talk—but, of the two, listening pays the finest, happiest dividends.

These are just a few of the mental and emotional attitudes that prevent people from getting along with one another.

It boils right down, in the last analysis, to the need for developing control of your mind and emotions. You will constantly have to adapt yourself to the changing moods of friends and loved ones. Don't let things they say or do, when they get disturbed, upset you. If you react in kind, you only make matters worse. Let the situation blow over. Play it down instead of up, or walk out on it until the atmosphere clears. Don't hold ill feelings or grudges. They will build up in you until you are tempted to blow your own top. If you remain master of yourself, you will be able to master conditions and others around you. Getting along harmoniously with others can be accomplished best by getting along with yourself first.

THOUGHTS TO BUILD INTO YOUR LIFE

To get along with others, I must develop the ability to adapt myself to their differences in temperament, personality, mental and emotional attitudes, likes and dislikes.

I cannot expect others to adapt themselves to me.

I resolve now, however, not to live in fear of what others may think of me.

I am assuming a "live and let live" policy.

I will not criticize or find fault with others. Instead, I will look for the good in them and things they are doing that I can commend.

As much as I care for my home, my personal possessions, the love I have for things—I will not put these ahead of people, of my dear ones.

I will keep from being self-centered by paying attention to the needs, desires and interests of others.

I will always remember that the best way to get along with others is to be able to get along with *myself!*

16

The Power of Mind in Healing

There is a creative power in mind which, properly directed, can heal you. I have used this power to heal different physical disturbances that have developed in me through wrong thinking, and you can learn to use it, too.

Cross-examine yourself! If you don't possess the degree of health you should have, what have you been doing to help create these disturbed conditions? You can be sure you've been doing something to upset the chemistry of your body by letting some fears, worries, hates or resentments run riot inside you. Nothing happens by accident. There are causes behind even the most insignificant things that occur. It's now an established fact that your body reflects the attitudes of your mind, if these attitudes become chronic. You well know that worry and apprehension can upset your digestion, cause your heart to palpitate, bring on a shortness of breath and nervous perspiration. A sudden fright can do all that. *I've emphasized this before,* so don't try to tell me that how you think and feel doesn't affect your health.

Now, note this important point: if your mind has the power to make you sick through wrong thinking it obviously has the power to make you well, to heal you, through *right* thinking!

I do not claim that the power of will, the creative power,

is a cure-all; but I *do* know that the *right* mental attitude will aid any person in ill health. This doesn't mean you can kid yourself by giving lip service to "Every day, in every way, I am getting better and better," when you are doing nothing to change wrong mental attitudes or habits or practices that have brought on ill health.

We all know people who are continually talking about backaches, headaches, stomach-aches or some other kind of aches. They harp on them, and the first thing they know, with that reiteration, the aches become realities. If you have such an ache or pain, if you've determined that it is nothing serious, just a nerve or tension reaction of some sort, there is no point in talking about it; neither is there any point to talking about your worries, your troubles. All this does is to aggravate yourself further, and irritate others. They have worries and troubles of their own they want to talk about, and they are apt to resent your beating them to the punch. And it's some punch, too—when you don't feel right, it hits you smack in the solar plexus. You go around with that hangdog, all-gone feeling, and the more you repeat how lousy you feel, the more certain you are that you should keep within reach of an undertaker. Constant reflection on your ills will magnify them and cement them to you.

Get away from the negative side and become an affirmative type. Think affirmatively, and the first thing you know, your aches, worries and troubles will disappear. They can't continue to live off you, if you refuse to give them nourishment.

A TREMENDOUS PHYSICAL COME-BACK!

A man wrote me recently from the coast and asked me to release him from a promise he had made to me. He had been paralyzed as the result of a car crash; his brain had been injured so that he had to learn to speak, to read and to spell all over again. He was brought in a wheelchair to my class in self-development, and could only utter unintelligible sounds for words, although he knew inwardly what he wanted to say. He was so emotionally disturbed and wanted to say what he felt so badly, that he tried to make his throat and tongue respond before they had been prepared.

My instruction to him was to see a "picture" in his mind's eye of every word he wished to speak, before he tried to create the sound of the word. I told him that I believed that by this method he would eventually recover his ability to talk. I also suggested to him that he *not* permit his thoughts to run together, that he should see pictures in his mind of every thought which came to him, taking it slowly and easily, like slow-motion pictures. It was my conviction that, as he regained command of his senses and his emotions, he could speed up this operation to normal.

"When you have learned to type and to spell again," I said, "I would like you to give me the thrill of writing your first letter to me!" He promised he would do this, but prior to the receiving of this letter which he had dictated to a friend a year had gone by. It read:

Dear Mr. Sherman:
    As you know, I promised to write my first letter to you. However, in the meantime, I have found out that I have a sister in Holland and *she* has asked me, when I am ready, to write her my *first* letter.
    I've said nothing until I ask you if you will release me. A promise is a promise. May I have your letter, releasing me? I can do nothing before I receive your letter. I know you will understand.
    I can talk almost perfectly now; I can read two-thirds; and I have just begun to spell all these thousands of words. I think when another year is finished, I should have everything back—reading, writing, spelling and speaking.

Of course, I released this man from his promise so that his sister could be the *first* to share in the knowledge of his triumph. I haven't permission to use his name and always treat such cases in confidence, holding them in anonymity, unless permission is granted for disclosure of the identities of such individuals. But what this man has done through his own heroic, mental efforts at self-rehabilitation, when doctors dismissed his condition as hopeless, is a modern miracle.

How well I recall that, after each class session, this man would grip my hand and make inarticulate sounds, telling me with his eyes how much he appreciated what he was getting from my talks, and how hard he was going to try to apply instructions given! He had begun to speak words before the class sessions of five nights were over, putting them into halting sentences!

In the presence of such achievements despite an impaired physical body, we who think we are handicapped should be shamed into a much greater effort to overcome our own weaknesses. The power of mind, rightly exercised, can do what otherwise would be impossible. If all else has seemingly failed, why not call upon your own God-given creative power within? You have only to *picture* what you want, persistently and with faith, and put forth every effort— and wonders can come to pass!

RECOVERY FROM A NERVOUS BREAKDOWN

There are many different kinds of nervous breakdowns, stemming from many different causes. But the basic causative forces are always a too-sensitized mental or emotional reaction to past life experiences. In the grip of such a nervous disturbance, you feel totally inadequate and incapable of facing certain situations in your present. It seems that your ego, your identity, the *real you,* is being buffeted from all sides. You try to run away from life, but wherever you take your physical body, seeking a change of scenery and a freedom from current associations, you discover that you have taken the mental and emotional condition along with you.

Ultimately, you decide that the only way to return to a normal state of mind and emotions is to face the music wherever you are, as you try to remove all discordant vibrations from your life.

Hundreds of people write me, during the course of a year, hoping that I may be able to give them some suggestions or techniques of right thinking that will produce in them the strength and the faith to get back on their mental and emotional feet. I am careful to state that I am not a doctor or a psychiatrist and that I have no desire or intent to supplant their services. However, ascertaining that they have received or are receiving medical or psychiatric treatment, I feel free to suggest mental attitudes they may assume as an aid to their recovery.

One such case had to do with a Mrs. B. from Australia. She had been suffering from a severe nervous condition that had persisted for years, and that had resisted all manner of medical and psychological approaches. A friend had finally given her one of my books, and she had written to tell me it had been helpful, leading her to hope that she might, somehow, be able to help herself. I answered, giving her every encouragement possible, because, when any individual decides that he or she is going to put forth the effort to "help themselves," good things can commence to happen!

Here, now, is the happy outcome of this woman's struggle to regain control of herself, told in her own words:

> Since I last wrote you, I have been *cured* of my nervous trouble. I have received therapy from a young man I met through a friend of mine who had also suffered a nervous breakdown. He *cured* me by going back over my childhood life (as you had suggested) experiences that I had undergone with my mother and explaining them all to me. I realized, then, that if I had given my mother my unlimited

affection I would have made her very happy and it would have relieved me of many guilt feelings and hostilities which had grown through the years.

I visited this young man every Monday evening for six months. He advised me to use the words *I am* in everything I did. For example, "*I am* peeling the potatoes," "*I am* hearing a dog bark" and so on . . . saying it under my breath, all the time, in everything I did. He explained that in this way I would avoid "confusion" in my thoughts. He was right. I did as he suggested on my daily rounds, and all my terrifying fears have gone forever. He also explained that use of *I am* would mean there is no "past" and no "future," *just this very moment.*

Your advice to me in your letters, Mr. Sherman, is so much along the same lines. My husband and I get along very well now, although I did not tell him of my lessons with the therapist. I know he would *never* understand my nervous breakdown or why I had it. But that does not matter to me, the wonderful thing is that I can enjoy life, *unafraid!*

THE HEALING POWER OF LOVE

Scientists at Harvard, under the direction of Professor Pitirim A. Sorokin, have conducted a most unusual experiment. Their research concerned the *power of love.* They discovered that love has more power over disease than medicine. Right doses of this emotion can produce longer life, greater health and happiness, as well as peace of mind. Young and old are transformed when the love potion is taken.

If you don't like somebody and have been burning yourself up hating him, start loving that person, and see what happens. You're apt to end up with a friend, instead of an enemy, and a stomach free of ulcers. Most human beings never forget an insult, but they remember a kindness even longer. Since like attracts like (ever hear this before?)

wouldn't you rather give out with love and kindness and get love and kindness back?

You've heard people say, "I'll get even with so-and-so if it takes the rest of my life!" Carrying such resentment around with them takes far more out of them than it does the person hated.

Everyone wants to be loved, even a dog; and everyone warms up to love, even a dog. You feel better when you love and are loved. Look at the dried-up men and women around you who are starved for love, if you think love isn't a mighty, creative, vital force! Several scientists have tried loving some plants and hating others, and the plants that were nourished with love have thrived while the plants poisoned by hate, but given the same mechanical care and watering, have been undersized or have even shriveled and died!

There's an old saying: "You can love a person to death"; but I'll take my chances any day on *love* against hate. Get the hate out of your life if you wish to attain and retain health!

FRUSTRATION A MENACE TO HEALTH

A frustrating or disillusioning experience can upset a person's health as quickly as a sudden, injurious accident. Your nervous system reacts immediately to mental and emotional shocks! If they continue, like the reverberations of an earthquake, they begin to affect your body chemistry and make you susceptible to a variety of ailments.

Remember my telling you in Chapter 14 of my unhappy experience with Mr. "X"? In the light of what I am going to say now, it might be well for you to turn back and reread this account.

It is just not possible to go through this life without suffering a certain amount of frustration and disillusionment. But it is *how* we react to these experiences, mentally and emotionally, which determines the degree of damage we may physically suffer as a consequence of these often tragic, disturbing happenings.

I confess to having my weak moments, despite the fact that I have known better. As prepared as I thought I was a few years ago to "take anything on the chin" and let it bounce off as though it were nothing at all, I was hit hard by the unwarranted faith I had placed in Mr. "X." I had conquered my feelings of hate and resentment against any person for any cause, thoroughly convinced of the harm they could do to me, mentally and physically, so I did not entertain any ill feeling toward this man. BUT, I let myself become so deeply hurt by reflection over the time and energy and money lost, and the involvement of respected friends in this "promising" venture, that these feelings began to do things to me. I felt, temporarily, so helpless to extricate myself from the situation in which I had been left, that my body took on a condition which duplicated, physically, what I was going through mentally. A violent attack of sciatica struck me, so painful that I could not walk and literally crawled about on my hands and knees for six weeks!

This was the most paralyzing experience of my life. Sympathetic friends said they were sending me "good thoughts." Several came to pray and volunteer mental treatments of one kind or another. I tried to be appreciative as well as cooperative, but I knew inwardly, until I could get over this "hurt" in my mind, the "hurt" in my body would persist—and it *did!*

When you have lived most of a lifetime with a dream, an aspiration, an ambition, and you have been led to believe its materialization was near at hand, only to have everything "blown away" practically overnight, you can have the best philosophy in the world and yet, under these testing conditions, encounter difficulty applying it.

210

I tell you this to let you know that none of us is invulnerable. I had not lost faith in myself or in the God Power within, but I *had* made the mistake of not going to work on myself at once to clear my consciousness of this severe disillusionment. Had I done this, not allowing myself to go over these unhappy events again and again in my mind, they could not have become deeply implanted in my subconscious.

Once these hurt feelings were so deeply imbedded, and reflecting themselves in an equally paining body, I had a major battle on my hands to overcome and eliminate the "two hurts." It was obvious to me that the "mental hurt" was feeding the "physical hurt" and keeping it alive. Even so, I was so concerned about the reshaping of my life and my plans, as a result of this "debacle," that I was temporarily unable to see my way out, and thus my condition was further aggravated.

Like the alcoholic who ultimately discovers that he must stop brooding about his past unhappy experiences, and place his faith in a Higher Power, I came back to the realization that I could not solve all my problems at once, and that I must begin where I should have begun at the start—with *myself.*

I came back to a declaration that I had found so serviceable in past trials and tribulations, and which I had mentioned in one or more of my books—a declaration that many readers had reported had been most helpful to them.

"*Nothing or no one can hurt me—unless I let them hurt me!*"

As simple as that! Repeat this to yourself and observe the feeling of inner power it gives you. It closes the door on all outside influences. It builds up a shielding wall inside. You sense that you are taking command of the situation. You call upon this Higher Power within, and you say to yourself:

"With God's help I am overcoming all conditions of mind and body that are not in harmony, that are out of order. I have nothing to fear. The future will take care of itself, so long as I take care of myself—so long as I control my thoughts and my feelings. I know that 'Nothing or no one can hurt me—unless I let them hurt me.' I now declare an end to my troubles, in the faith that, with a clear mind, I will find an answer to all problems. I am free of all feelings of hate or resentment, any and all destructive thoughts. I am completely well in body and in mind—capable of meeting any situation in life as it should be met."

When I administered these thoughts to myself, it was the dose of medicine I had needed all along. Believing them, I felt their impact on my mind as well as my body. After repeating them in meditative periods during the day and night, I suddenly felt a mental and physical release. The hurt was gone from my consciousness and the pain was gone from my body. I arose from my bed as though nothing had ever happened to me, and have had no recurrence since.

SPIRITUAL HEALINGS ARE POSSIBLE

In two of my former books *How to Use the Power of Prayer* and *How to Make ESP Work for You*, I have reported documented cases of "spiritual healings" that have been performed by my friend, the Reverend Harold Hayward of California, through use of "prayer therapy." He has graciously responded to requests from many readers for his prayers on their behalf. In many instances, unusual and undoubted healings have occurred.

Mr. Hayward prefers, if possible, a personal contact with the afflicted individual, so that he can place his hands on the affected part of the body, while praying. A little-understood "healing form of energy" seems to be transmitted, as though faith provides a substance in the process of spiritual meditation. Science still cannot explain exactly what happens when a "mental healing" is accomplished.

One of his most recent successes has just been reported to me at my request. A Mrs. Toenjes, whom I had met on a previous trip to California, came to him, complaining of severe pain in her chest and a swelling on her right side. "She had been to her doctor," stated Mr. Hayward, "who told her he suspected a growth and made an appointment with the UCLA Medical Center for a complete examination to ascertain the extent of her illness.

"I put my hands on her chest and prayed for her. I felt the swelling disappear, and she said the pain and soreness had gone.

"The enclosed letter which came yesterday (April 5, 1965) tells its own story and can be verified, of course, through the UCLA Medical Center."

The enclosure, signed by Mrs. Toenjes, is now in my files. Addressed to Mr. Hayward, it reads:

> Hello
>
> I am sorry I did not write sooner to tell you how good I feel about my healing. I have no pain or soreness since you prayed for me, although, to please one of the girls and neighbors, I went to UCLA for a check. *There was nothing they could find. . . .*

The healing had taken place on March 29th. Mrs. Toenjes concluded:

> This is the first time in fifteen years either of us has been sick. We are feeling real good today and we thank God for such a good and true friend as you, and what you have done for me.

It is not the words that Mr. Hayward uses when he prays; it is the feeling of conviction and of absolute faith that he puts behind the words. He has now had such varied and successful experiences in the realm of prayer that he can almost instantly assume and maintain the right mental and emotional attitude when praying.

I have asked him if it is necessary to perform a "laying on of hands" every time a healing prayer is offered. He says that it is not, although he thinks that, when it is convenient, physical contact may be more effective. The touch may mean much to an afflicted person, who is better able to picture a cure when he feels a hand upon the injured or afflicted area.

"To some people," explains Mr. Hayward, "placing a hand upon the head or another part of the body is like a benediction. It helps them get into the mood to join in prayer for their recovery. It is as though some kind of a circuit is closed between the two of us and the God Power within us. Once an individual really senses this, an instantaneous healing often takes place. They always testify that they feel much better, and progress usually continues until they are well."

Mr. Hayward makes no claim that he is able to achieve 100 percent results. But his successes over the years have far outnumbered his failures. Science needs to make a profound study of "faith healing." This is one of the areas that I intend to have my ESP Foundation research. I am convinced that the more we can attain and maintain contact with the God Power within, the better we will be in every way.

WHAT EMOTIONAL BITTERNESS CAN DO

Of the hundreds of cases I have known wherein men and women incurred severe physical ailments by chronically nursing bitter feelings over tragic past experiences, none is more dramatically illustrative than the self-created condition of a woman we will call "Mrs. Dawson."

Another wheelchair case, she came to my class in New York City several years ago. She was an *arthritic cripple.*

Her hands were badly misshapen. She heard me say that *wrong thinking*—hate, resentment, bitterness—could so charge the system with destructive impulses as to change the chemistry of the body and bring on physical ills such as arthritis and rheumatism. She waited after the lecture to see me. Then she said, defiantly:

"Did you mean to imply that *I* have brought this condition on myself?"

"It's entirely possible," I answered, "if you have been emotionally disturbed about something in life, if someone has done something to you that you can't forget or forgive, if you've brooded about it, if you haven't been able to get it out of your consciousness. If these feelings are still pent up within you, then they have had to seek some outlet—some form of expression—because every thought *must* take some external form in some way—this is the law. Your arthritis may therefore be the physical reflection of the disturbed thoughts and feelings you have carried around for years."

The woman burst into tears.

"I haven't wanted to confess it," she said, "but it's true. I *am* full of bitterness. I can't ever forgive my son for what he's done to his father and to me. He turned out to be a criminal—he's serving a life sentence in the penitentiary for having killed a man. He disgraced us so, we had to sell a home we had saved and sacrificed thirty years to buy. We had to leave the community where we lived and go to a strange city where we weren't known. I'm in New York visiting relatives at present but I can't believe—it doesn't seem right that I should suffer like this because of something my son did!"

"It's possible, madam," I said to her, "that *you* have contributed, unintentionally, to your boy's turning out to be a criminal!"

"How can you *say* a thing like that?" she demanded.

I asked her to review her early life with her boy. She told me he had always been headstrong, wanted his own way. His father was a traveling salesman and had little time for his son. The boy got into some local troubles of a minor nature with the wrong crowd. She worried, scolded, tried to keep him in nights and warned him he would end up a criminal. She confessed she used to lie awake nights, month after month, worrying, *picturing* the worst happening. Sure enough, things *did* get worse and worse—until the son went out with a gang and shot someone in a robbery attempt.

His deed brought lasting disgrace on the family. Mrs. Dawson couldn't face it in the same community. Even today, when she thought of her son, it was with bitterness. But, having told me all this, the mother began to *see* what her wrong thinking had done—not only to her, but to the boy. Turning to me, she said, appealingly: "How can I *undo* all this now—is it—*too late?*"

"It's too late to undo some of it," I replied, "but you can start by writing to your son and asking for *his* forgiveness, and you can forgive *him* for what you have felt he has done to you. You can resolve that you are going to do everything possible to make up to your boy, and everyone concerned, for the mistakes you have made and the bitterness you have held."

"If I *do* this," asked the woman, "and I don't know whether I can or not—I've felt this way so long—but IF I do this, do you think I will get better *physically?*"

"You can't help but get better," I assured her, "when you stop pouring poison into your system through wrong thinking and start replacing hate with love—something is bound to happen. How *big* a change will occur will depend upon *you.*"

This woman went to work on herself. She adjusted the bitter, unhappy situation between her son and herself. The lifting of this load *alone* did something tremendous to her spirit, her mental attitude, her emotions. In *three and a half months* from that day, she left her wheelchair. Today, while she understandably does not want her real name to be known, she is free of arthritis except for a few of the scars, and she is devoting much of her time to helping others correct their wrong thinking.

What are *your* feelings doing to *you*? If your health isn't what it should be, if your life is unhappy or unsettled, go back in your mind to some time and experience which has upset you emotionally, and get these feelings out of your system. Don't delay!

Mental healing is now an established fact in many types of physical disorders, particularly as they relate to the nervous system. Doctors and surgeons readily admit the value of a patient's mental attitude in all cases of sickness. There are physical limitations, of course, since we are living in a physical universe. And it is obviously not possible for a person who has lost a leg or an arm to grow a new one by mentally picturing it. But where the body is still intact, where nerve centers have been impaired but not destroyed, where vital organs are yet capable of functioning, the influence of your inner or subconscious mind can be a great and deciding factor in your recovery.

The use of your mind in combating disease and overcoming physical and nervous disorders is a comparatively new and uncharted field in the operation of human consciousness. Some religions have been founded on this faculty of mind and many claims have been made by New Thought advocates. Holy shrines have their yearly quota of thousands allegedly "cured."

It is wise, always, to consult a competent physician . . . but it is also advisable to aid the physician by assuming the proper mental attitude toward your condition. More important, if you see to it that wrong mental pictures of fear and worry are removed from consciousness, you will do much to preserve your youth and your health.

Proof that the mind has a tremendous effect upon the body has been obtained through experiments in hypnotism. Doctors have found that subjects, directed under hypnosis, can control their blood supply, change their heartbeat, make themselves immune to pain, can have needles and knives put through their bodies without drawing blood or leaving a mark, and can hold crushing weights on their abdomens and chests made rigid through mental suggestion.

This indicates the amazing power of your subconscious mind when it is properly reached and directed. It demonstrates the influence you can exert upon your body by consciously picturing the existence of health, so that your subconscious can convey this impression to every part of your physical being.

Dare to live. Have the courage to face life as you have encountered it. Obey all ordinary physical laws—moderation in eating, drinking, sleeping, working and exercise.

NEVER give up hope. If physicians have pronounced the "death sentence" upon you, then you must place full dependence upon faith and the God-given healing power within you. Under these circumstances, it may be possible for you so to activate the cells of your body by your own right thinking, that a healing will take place. Put your trust in meditation and prayer. Thousands of men and women have been miraculously restored to health and vigor after all hope was apparently gone. What they have been able to do should greatly bolster your own hope and faith!

THOUGHTS TO BUILD INTO YOUR LIFE

I possess a healing power in my consciousness which can restore me to health and keep me well in body and mind.

This healing power responds to the nature and character of my thoughts and feelings. If I am disturbed, dominated by fears and worries, this will cause me to present mental pictures of illness to my subconscious which will prevent the healing power from functioning.

I must get away from the negative and become an affirmative type, if I would eliminate my aches and worries and troubles.

I must refuse to permit disillusionment in others, betrayal of confidence, advantage taken in a business deal, and various human frailties to upset me mentally and emotionally. If I do, I know that these reactions can affect me, physically and mentally, and bring on ill health.

Regardless of any physical condition that I may ever have to face, I will never give up hope and the faith that It can be healed.

Science and religion are united in the realization today that the mind can and does have a great influence on the body, and that doctors and patients, working together, often achieve miracles.

219

17

The Power to Face Advancing Age

No doubt you have had cause to realize that "age" is an increasing problem in American life . . . in the life of the world. Men and women are living years longer than they did half a century ago thanks to the advances of medical science and better ways of living. This very fact of greater longevity, however, has produced mounting economic problems.

Our entire concept of "age" is wrong and must be changed. We have associated with the idea of "age" the belief that "age" in itself means physical and mental incapacity, that no older person is capable of being useful to society. Actually, many men and women in advancing years still possess *good body* and *sound mind* and are just as well equipped to continue in active service as they were when years younger. Even more so, these years have given them an experience and a skill, a maturity of judgment which younger men and women have not yet acquired. And yet, by law as well as by the mandates of pension and other retirement plans instituted by business and industry, such older men and women are usually compelled to give up good-paying positions upon reaching the age of sixty-five or sixty, and to go literally "upon the shelf."

One day they are gainfully and happily employed, enjoying economic security, and the very next day, after arrival at the designated age limit, they are out of work, dependent upon a usually inadequate pension or Old Age Assistance payments and Social Security, which often are not sufficient, unless there are other resources to draw upon, to enable them to maintain the standard of living they have earned and enjoyed all their lives.

Many businesses and industries operate on a retirement plan and will not hire men and women over forty or forty-five, because persons over these ages cannot pay *in* enough money out of their wages to entitle them to retirement pay. Some employers feel a great sympathy for older persons who apply for work and would like to hire them, but the arbitrary regulations set up by the companies prohibit such employment. And, of course, there are many businesses and industries that have no retirement plan but, never-theless, are committed to the hiring of younger persons. This is the era of youth—and it has become, unhappily, the era of youth *against* age. How can the million and more teen-agers graduating from high school each year be ab-sorbed into the labor market? Young people find it difficult to comprehend that they will be the older people of tomor-row. If they could, they would be more generous and under-standing of the problems now being faced by their elders.

YOU MUST ADAPT TO THIS CHANGING ORDER!

If you are in the older age brackets, you must give thought to new ways in which you can adapt yourself to change—and see to it that you remain *young in spirit!* Such an atti-tude can keep you well and active and better able to cope with economic problems.

One woman wrote me that since her hair had turned white, she couldn't get a job, even though she had been a highly skilled office manager, shorthand stenographer and receptionist. Finally, in desperation, she had her hair dyed black, started to wear younger style dresses and immediately secured a fine-paying position as hostess in a big hotel dining room.

"Of course, I lied about my age on the application," she confessed. "I didn't feel good about that but friends said I looked twenty years younger; I felt it, too, when I saw the reaction my new appearance was having on all whom I met. Do you know, this change has brought me new romance as well? It's too bad a person has to falsify today, to qualify. But that's the kind of a world in which we are living, I guess."

Yes, there are many inequities which apply to older people today. Many feel they are being neglected, shunted aside, left to shift, almost helplessly, for themselves, by former business associates, friends and relatives.

"The only sin we have committed is living too long," one oldster said to me. "In my case, if I had died years ago and left what I possess to my children and their children my memory would have been revered. But now, as I live on from year to year, gradually using up my life savings, which might have gone to them, I can tell that they resent my continued existence. They can see that, if I don't die soon, I won't have a thing left to pass on to them. It's a great shock to me to realize that they have cared more for my possessions than they've cared for me. And yet, I've always been generous with what I've had; I've never denied my children what I thought was good for them. I saw to it that all four had a good education and were established in life on his or her own. But still they want more—they want me out of the way—the sooner, the better, while I still have something in the bank!"

This pretty grim picture is one which applies in varying

degrees to many family situations today. An aged woman confided that she had thought she was dying a few years ago and had called in her three grown children and made a division of her property. Then, when she miraculously recovered, she found herself a pauper, compelled to seek relief, for her children would not return to her what had been given—or wait for this division to take place until she actually died.

"Now I know they had counted on getting hold of what I had, the instant I passed on," she said, "and once they had gotten my money from me, they no longer pretended that they even cared for me!"

What unhappiness money and the coveting of the possessions of others can cause!

Haven't you heard people say: "So-and-so is an old bore and a pain in the neck. But he or she is a relative of mine and I've got to put up with him or her because I suppose I'm going to be left something when he or she dies!"

If you are a parent or grandparent and have some money and property which is to go to your children and their children when you die, it might be wise to end all speculation by telling them just how you intend to care for them in your will. If you are sure you have enough to live on the rest of your life, you might better make a property settlement while you are still alive, retaining enough for yourself, so that you can have the satisfaction of seeing your relatives enjoy your bequests and also be on hand to make sure that no selfish or jealous family feuds grow out of what you have divided among them.

Human greed being what it is, you must be prepared for disillusionment concerning the reactions of some relatives who may have professed deep affection for you. By facing "older age" realistically, you will save yourself some severe emotional shocks.

HOW ABOUT AN OLD PEOPLE'S HOME?

The following letter is typical of many I receive:

Dear Mr. Sherman:
Do you think I would be happy in an Old People's Home? I am getting to the age where I may need physical care and I do not want to be a burden upon my grown children and their families.

(Mrs. J. G.)

A typical answer that I make to such questions is as follows:

It depends upon the Old People's Home. Some such institutions have a high type of men and women as residents, whose companionship is most enjoyable. In such surroundings you could make a new, interesting life for yourself.

It would be well, however, for you to visit several homes for the aged, if you possess sufficient resources, to judge for yourself whether or not you could be happy in these institutions.

Companionship in your later years means almost as much as the physical care you might receive. In many instances it means more, because if you are not at least mentally happy, it becomes doubly hard to bear any possible physical infirmities or disabilities.

Sparing your relatives the burden of your care is a fine, unselfish resolution. Wherever possible, if an older person can retain his or her independence, even partially, it is much better for all concerned and makes for happier family relations all around.

CAN YOU LIVE ALONE AND LIKE IT?

As you grow older, and lifetime friends and relatives depart, including, perhaps, your husband or wife, you may find yourself living alone or by yourself most of the time. This may or may not constitute a major problem, depending on whether or not you mind being alone, whether or not you are good company for yourself, whether or not such time-consuming interests as radio, television, the movies, good books, trips and other diversions are satisfying substitutions for lack of human companionship.

It is probable these activities will lose much of their savor participated in alone, because you have been accustomed in the past to sharing them with others. The company of an understanding, congenial person of similar interests and tastes is almost a "must" to keep life from becoming a deadly bore.

It is a rare individual who can live with himself, by himself. One must be an extremely introspective type (so self-centered that he creates a world of his own and lives in his reflected image), or else possess a philosophy of life which gives him the inner assurance of attunement with Nature and with God.

I have met some of the latter type who are far from hermits. The radio has kept them well informed, some have done considerable reading and, once you get to know them, they will enter into discussions of what's wrong or right with mankind, the country and the world, handing out comments and advice which often would do credit to supposed "learned people."

One elderly man, gnarled and bent with his ninety-three years of age and his exposure to the out-of-doors, resides in a weather-beaten one-room house not many miles from me. He came to this region in northern Arkansas more than sixty years ago and homesteaded where he now lives. "I married a girl in Wisconsin, had a quarrel the first week, walked out the door and kept on walking and ended up here," he told me. "Haven't seen or heard from her since and I haven't wanted anything more to do with a woman. But I wouldn't take a million for this dog of mine."

Apart from this slightly warped viewpoint, the oldster's

views on world affairs are rational and pertinent. But whether we live alone or not, we're all a little one-sided or "overboard" on some subjects, depending on our reaction to the experiences which have come to us in life.

Man, as a creature, wasn't made to live alone. A philosopher once said: "God made the two sexes so that man and woman would have to seek each other to gain a sense of completeness—and to fulfill the inborn desire for a loving, understanding companionship."

If some of us haven't found our rightful mate, we have had to make an emotional adjustment in order to realize happiness alone.

The most lonely people I have ever met have not been those who are living by themselves, removed from civilization, but men and women who are out of harmony with relatives or friends and, though surrounded by people and activities, are wretchedly unhappy.

Usually, the man or woman who can live with himself or herself has the capacity to live happily with others. But, as in the case of the ninety-three-year-old man, some kind of companionship is necessary—if it is only the company of a faithful dog.

If you are lonely or alone, and in your later years, start doing something about it. Begin by taking an interest in things outside yourself and in other people. Since "like attracts like" (never, never forget this!) you will soon have others showing a friendly interest in *you!*

CULTIVATE YOUNGER PEOPLE AS FRIENDS

To avoid being left on an "island" from which all those your age have departed on the long voyage of "no return," seek the friendship and company of men and women of the younger generation. You can bridge the difference in ages by maintaining a youthful spirit and a sincere interest in their activities. It will help to know that you can still count on their companionship should you outlive most, if not all, in your age bracket.

In a recent meeting of the Lions Club of Mountain View, Arkansas, of which I am a member, the District Governor of the Lions commented that the membership should be comprised of young, middle-aged and older men. He said the young Lions could supply the *energy* to get civic jobs done; the middle-aged could supply the *stability* and then, looking in my direction, he said, "the *older* members can supply the *wisdom*."

Now, I have never considered myself as "old" . . . or even "older." Or, any wiser! Just the same, it comes as a shock to me to hear some people begin referring to me as "Old Man Sherman." I am sure that I do not *think* old or *act* old. And when I hear some of the citizens referring to a prominent woman as "Old Lady So-and-So," I feel like protesting. Neither you nor I need to accept these concepts of age, especially if we feel ourselves to be vigorous in mind and body.

Not long ago I went cave exploring with men thirty and forty years my junior. We had to be lowered with a rope around the waist, almost a hundred feet, down a chimney-like hole in the top of a mountain. For some hours, it was the most rugged kind of going—over great piles of rubble and the jagged rock deposits of centuries, crawling on hands and knees through narrow crevices and tunnels, ascending steep cliffs more than a hundred feet high and covered with a slippery clay coating in which were only the barest of hand and foot holds. Taxing on physical endurance as well as nerves, this was accomplished in pitch-black darkness, broken only by the carbide lights on our steel helmets.

When men my age, who said they wouldn't have gone down into this cave (one of the biggest in the world, bigger than the famous Carlsbad Caverns) for a million dollars, asked me why I had risked possible serious injury on such an adventure, I answered simply: "I didn't think of my age as having anything to do with it. I just wanted to see the wonders of Nature in this vast Blanchard Springs Caverns area, and I was so fascinated with every step of this underground exploration, that I had no thought of danger!"

I am sure, looking back, that a spirit of warm camaraderie was established among all who went down into this cave together; although we all emerged exhausted from this somewhat hazardous trip, the happy experience that we shared with each other will live in our memories as though we were all of one age—the age of eternal youth.

Now, of course, you probably have no nearby cave to explore, as a means of furthering fellowship with the younger generation. But if you possess reasonable mental and physical health, there are many community and social activities wherever you live that will give you opportunity for such association.

It is a mistake to retire to the rocking chair as long as you can contribute your services and your lifetime experiences in some manner. Sharing them is the one way left to you to keep young and to enjoy the feeling of usefulness, of worthwhileness. And when you look into the eyes of younger men and women and see respect and regard for you ashine in them, you will sense a glow of inner satisfaction in the certain knowledge that you are wanted and appreciated.

CONCERNING THE FEAR OF DEATH

Yes, a time that each of us must face in his own way is approaching—the time of departure from this world. We are fortunate indeed if we can retain our physical and mental health until the moment of transition comes. But many of us, no matter what fine care we take of ourselves, develop infirmities of body and of mind. These must be borne as courageously and uncomplainingly as possible.

You may have a religious belief that is sustaining you. If you have found, however, that your faith is faltering, that you cannot believe as you once did, that you no longer can accept the possibility of a life after death, you may be facing the future with deep apprehension, dread and fear.

Based upon extrasensory experiences I have had and research I have conducted, I now have the conviction that we *do* survive death. I perhaps cannot pass on my conviction to you with whatever I might say. You will have to find this inner assurance for yourself. But I know men and women who have developed the ability to leave their physical bodies *at will* and, while occupying body forms that have a higher rate and character of vibration (and therefore are invisible to the physical eyesight and ordinarily beyond the range of perception of the five physical senses), are able to visit what is termed "the next dimension." Here they find a world as seemingly *real* as this one is to us. Here they make contact with discarnate entities and repor visits with loved ones who have "gone on."

It is my expectation that, when scientific research can be conducted with such men and women as subjects, evidential proof of "survival" can be obtained. If this seems too incredible to you now, please "leave the jury out," keep an open mind, because what seemed totally impossible yesterday is being demonstrated today as within the realm of possibility.

Wouldn't it make a great difference to you, in your advancing age, to know beyond a doubt, that death of the body only liberates your soul, your identity, the "I am I" of you, to a higher existence? Wouldn't it challenge you to change your mental attitudes in preparation for such a continuing adventure? Wouldn't it cause you to wish to give a better account of yourself in the time left to you on this earth?

I think it would. Personally, I don't want to carry any useless baggage over into the next life. I know I will take with me only what I have developed here. That's all any of us will take.

Try as best you can to accept the changes in your body as they come. The fleshly house which you are now occupying has given you faithful service. Perhaps you have often mistreated it with excessive habits and appetites, with damaging thoughts and feelings. Be grateful to it as you would express gratitude to a trusting, faithful servant.

You were not created to live an eternity on this earth. It is only through physical death that you can be freed to another existence.

Have no fear. Live your life a day at a time, fully, and as happily as possible. Accept what you cannot help as graciously and as calmly and serenely as you can. And know that the God Presence within is just as near to you as it is to any other living creature any time, anywhere, throughout the boundless universe. This should be abiding inner assurance that, whatever happens, all will fundamentally be well with you.

THOUGHTS TO BUILD INTO YOUR LIFE

I accept the realistic fact that I am living in a changing world and that, as I grow older, I must face increasing problems of adjustment and adaptation.

I am aware that there are many problems of an economic, social and health nature which come with aging.

It is wise for me to anticipate these changes and to prepare for them as best I can, as early as I can.

It may be necessary or advisable for me to live alone, if I can afford it, and to avoid living with relatives, unless bad health compels dependence.

Even then, if a hospital or institution or Senior Citizens Home is available, it is preferable to involving the personal lives of close friends or loved ones, who have a right to their own privacy, however much they may care for me.

As long as I possess average health and vigor at any age, I will take part in all activities of a community and social nature which are not too taxing and which, at the same time, keep my interest in things that are going on about me and in the world, vital and alive.

I accept on faith that this life is not the end. On this assumption, I am giving more and more time and thought toward developing a philosophy which will enable me to face the change called death, without fear.

18

Danger in Misuse of TNT!

Now that you are ready to release this power within, the time has come to warn you what NOT to do in the handling of it!

You are actually dealing with a high explosive—wrong use of TNT can wreck your life. Not only your life but the lives of all you hold dear.

This is because you have been created a creature of free will and free choice, and you can choose to use this power for evil as well as for good. If you take the path of evil, you do so at your own peril.

Millions of human beings have destroyed themselves by so doing, and millions more will do so before man thoroughly understands and gains control of this power in his life. This is the *crime of the ages*—that man has required so many untold centuries to even begin to gain an understanding of himself and this God-given power which, rightly used, could long ago have brought man lasting peace and happiness, prosperity and health and everything good man could ever have desired!

Today, wrong thinking, pent-up hates, resentments, greeds, fears, prejudices and other destructive feelings in all races of people are leading, inexorably, unless released by some miracle of new understanding of self and others, to the Cataclysm of the Ages!

You can only hold this power in leash for so long, for it *must* manifest itself in some form, good or bad, in this outer world! Look about you. View the widespread unrest, the human suffering and privation in many countries, the economic pressures, the violent hatreds and prejudices, the mounting ill-will, the wars and rumors of wars—all man-made, through *man's wrong thinking!*

What can be done about it? How can this highly dangerous misuse of TNT be stopped, to avert unspeakable destruction of man and all he holds dear?

Something must be done! And you must be the one to do it! Action can no longer wait upon others. It must start with *you*. Every mind that is using this power as it should be used is adding something positive and constructive to universal thought. You can have great influence among your own friends and loved ones and in your community. Be realistic in your approach, without being negative.

Whatever is to come, you can gain a great degree of guidance and protection for yourself by the right use of your own mind here and now. Actually, the power of mind to liberate or destroy man should be shouted to the housetops. *The most tremendous educational program in all world history should be launched to reveal to man what he is doing . . . to himself!*

History is replete with men who started out to use the power and were fast becoming headliners because of it. Then they succumbed to the temptation to use the power for selfish purposes, to take advantage of others, to gain domination over them. And although they succeeded for a time—some of them in a worldwide way—they all came to a tragic end. I have only to mention again such men as Nero, Julius Caesar, Mussolini, Hitler, Stalin, Lenin. . . . Think of all the misery they brought to humanity, the power they once had, and how the evil they created through misuse of this power has lived after them, in some instances, even down through the ages!

Watch your own use of this power! Don't let your ego expand as you find this power begins to elevate you!

Listen to the voice of your conscience! Ask yourself before each step you plan to take: "Am I making right use of this power? Am I employing it in a way that will bring harm to someone else or to me? Am I trying to advance too fast, before I am ready for the responsibilities and opportunities and experiences I am attracting?"

MAKE PROGRESS SLOWLY BUT SURELY!

Yes, it is possible for you to gain success—temporary success—too quickly. This power within doesn't have the ability to analyze or to determine your fitness to handle what you want in the right way, when you get it. All it has the ability to do is to deliver to you what you instruct it to deliver, through the kind of mental pictures you give it. You must be the judge as to whether or not you are equal to the demands you make upon the power within or it will produce results for you to which you cannot live up!

You know yourself better than any other person knows you. You know what you can and cannot do, within certain limitations. You know, for instance, if you are just out of college, that you will still have to balance your education with experience, that you can't start out at the head of a business or industry. You know that you can't succeed on the strength of your diploma alone. I hope you know *this* much! But I have talked to hundreds of college men and women who have failed in business, who have not made a success of their lives, who have gone out into the world with the feeling that the world now owed them a living— that their education qualified them for anything they wanted. They operated this power, with the aid of a pleasing personality, to get into responsible positions; they went along swimmingly for awhile until their lack of experience began to catch up with them. Then they began to feel the pressure. They became less sure of themselves—they saw other men and women, with less education but more experience, climbing ahead of them. They couldn't take it, they grew jealous, resentful and finally apprehensive. What was wrong? They had everything, and yet it didn't seem to count for much in the world of reality, in the battle of life! Perhaps education itself must share part of the blame. Perhaps youth has been taught to expect too much at the start.

Know yourself. Know what you want, but be honest—seek only what you feel you can handle. Picture yourself working to *earn* the right to possess what you are desirous of attaining. Don't wish upon yourself more than you are capable of doing at any time. You will grow naturally into finer and bigger opportunities, and the power within, in addition to your own efforts, will supply you with everything you need to get where you want to go, step by step up the ladder of success and happiness.

NEVER USE THE POWER FOR SELFISH PURPOSES!

It is a temptation to many people, coming into an awareness of this power for the first time, to attempt to use it for selfish purposes. The power will respond to your bidding, to whatever mental pictures you give it, whether your intentions are good or bad. You can picture taking advantage of some individual, and if you work toward that end, and if that person is too trusting and not alert to your design, you may be able to put it over on him. But in so doing, you have created a *susceptibility*—a vibration in your own consciousness which may attract to you that very same happening!

By such wrong manipulation of mind, you can, therefore, catch yourself in your own trap. What you plan to do to others, you are, without realizing it, really plotting to do to yourself because "your own always comes back to you."

Are you willing to earn what you desire in life by your own efforts? What you gain, without effort, without deserving, you usually lose just as quickly. This is because the magnetic force that has attracted it is not sustained; little or no power has been built up around anything that has come to you in an unmerited manner (through wrong operation of mind), and consequently someone else, with wrong use of power, can take it away from you.

Like, remember, always attracts like. *If you don't want someone to do something to you, don't do it first to him!* This is a paraphrase of an old admonition, but a word to the unwise should be the beginning of wisdom! You can't get away with anything in mind, eventually. The law of compensation will see to that.

Up to now, only a small percentage of human beings, at any one time, have ever rightly used this TNT. But every time they have, it has brought them great personal happiness, achievement, health, prosperity and even fame! The degree of happiness, achievement, health, prosperity and fame they have realized has been in proportion to the degree of use they have made of this power. This will always be so! Turn on a water faucet halfway; you will only get half the flow of water. Let only part of the power flow through you, and you diminish the returns it can bring to you.

Leaders who light the fuse of TNT by inflaming the hatreds and resentments and suspicions of great masses of people can wreak untold damage. Witness the Genghis Khans, Napoleons, Kaiser Wilhelms and Hitlers of history! There are always millions ready to be led for one who is willing and ready to lead . . . and to lead in the right direction! Mankind, as you know, has a tragic record of crucifying its saviors.

THE TIME FOR THE RIGHT USE OF MIND POWER IS AT HAND

But the time is at hand for man to recognize and accept, irrespective of his religious or philosophic beliefs, his race or color, the spiritual power within him—"that something" —which each man possesses and which, rightly directed, can bring to *all men* the peace and happiness and plenty and universal brotherhood that man has so long been seeking.

It's *here,* right inside you, a part of you just as it was in me, years ago, when I didn't realize, hadn't awakened to what I had, to what had always been mine, to what has always been in the world, available to all men in all ages— the treasure beyond all other treasures, the Holy Grail, the wisdom, the intelligence, the answer to all problems, but the curse of all curses, the most fiendish of all forces, if exploded in the wrong way by *man's wrong thinking!*

It's yours to use or misuse. Now that you have it and know how to operate it, what are you going to do with it?

How you decide to use it, at any time, will change your world and may change the whole world!

Danger: high explosive! Proceed with wisdom and caution.

"If you believe it, it is so!" But *what* do you believe?

What you believe, and what the people of this world believe, will make the world of tomorrow! And the TNT of these beliefs will *rock the earth!*

THOUGHTS TO BUILD INTO YOUR LIFE

I am mindful that if TNT is used wrongly this miraculous power within me can wreck my life.

Rightly used, I know that the power of TNT can bring me great peace of mind, a new and lasting sense of security, better economic conditions, permanent happiness and good health.

To maintain control of this TNT, I must remain humble in success and adversity—always asking myself before each important step I plan to take: "Am I making the right use of this power?"

I know that what I believe and what the people of the world believe, will make the world of tomorrow.

My faith in the functioning of this God-given creative power of TNT assures me of the guidance and protection I need to see me safely through whatever is to come.

19

Questions and Answers Concerning the Use of "That Something"

Through the years I have received many questions from men and women who have discovered "that something" within, the creative power of mind, and have been earnestly applying themselves to its study and use in their daily lives. Because some of these questions may be the very ones you would ask, I have selected the most representative to answer in this chapter with the hope that my answers will aid your further development and realization.

How can I keep my mind free from upsetting, weak, fear and worry thoughts that come to me seemingly from outside?

Wrong emotional reactions to different experiences you have had have implanted in your mind fears that similar experiences may come to you. Subconsciously, because of these fears, anything that has happened to you which is suggestive of former unhappy experiences produces these "upsetting, weak, fear and worry thoughts," as you describe them. The way to eliminate them is to release from your mind the emotional hold that past fears and worries have over you. As you do this, the power of these wrong thoughts to attract similar thoughts and reactions is proportionately reduced. In other words, the more you develop the *positive* attitude of mind, the less will you be influenced or disturbed by negative thoughts.

How can we have faith and ignore the fact that an enemy may be stalking us, ready to attack, or that the road we are following in the darkness may end in a precipice or that water we are about to drink may contain pernicious germs? Few of us have developed the power of premonition so that it can be depended upon in emergencies or everyday life.

Blind faith is always dangerous and is often worse than no faith at all. Real faith possesses an "inner knowing quality" about it. Such faith is based upon an intelligent awareness of the factors upon which you are basing your faith. You are not using your intelligence when you proceed without caution into an area where you may encounter an enemy, or come upon a precipice or possibly infested water. Faith was never intended as a substitute for intelligent action. It was and is designed to augment your intelligence, to activate the creative powers within to attract what you want and need to you, in association with your own efforts in that direction.

If you picture in mind, with faith, that you can safely avoid or meet an encounter with the enemy, or be guided without mishap along a road in the darkness, or be forewarned when you are about to do anything harmful such as the drinking of contaminated water, the creative power within follows your orders and gives you the "hunches," the impulses, urges and premonitions that serve to protect you.

You say that, in case of great danger, the subconscious makes us choose the right move. Yet, everybody, including myself, knows cases of people who, caught in a fire, have

240

abandoned their most precious belongings, while dragging out worthless pieces of furniture—or they have run the wrong way when the right way was open. How do you account for this?

Your subconscious will not "choose the right move" for you in an emergency, unless prepared by *right thinking* to do so! If you have always been afraid of fire and have not pictured what you would do in case of fire, you will be paralyzed by that fear when you find yourself caught in a fire, unable to receive any right direction from your subconscious. Remember: what comes out of your mind is only that which has gone into it at some previous time . . . because you have created your world by your own past reaction to it. In your desire to save something from the fire, because you have never pictured the things worth saving in event of fire, you hysterically grab up anything. Because you have never pictured what exits you would take in case of fire, you have only one frenzied thought—to get out—not the *way* to get out! Start now in preparing your mind to meet any emergency.

I do a great amount of traveling, stopping in all types of motels and hotels. I have no fear of fire, but as an intelligent precaution, the first thing I do upon arriving at my destination is locate the exits nearest my room, the positions of the fire escapes and stairways. I even test the fire-escape doors to see if they happen to be locked, or windows leading onto fire escapes, to determine if they may be jammed. (In many instances I have found conditions that would not have permitted escape—such as locked doors and windows that would not open.) I picture in my mind the layout of the room and whether a right or left turn, on leaving it, takes me to the nearest exit, so that I could find it in the dark if necessary. This checkup and observation takes me five to ten minutes, then I dismiss it from my conscious mind, knowing that if a fire should break out, I will instantly be made aware of the right moves to make. In addition, I decide just what articles I will take with me so that I won't be confused in trying to determine this during a fire, when my mind needs to be free to meet the existing situation. Your subconscious, "that something" within, will never fail you if you properly instruct it and liberate your consciousness from fear.

You say the subconscious is all-intelligent and practically infallible, if I understand you correctly. Then how can the subconscious be influenced by wrong, unwarranted or pernicious thoughts or happenings, from outside?

Suggestion! Your subconscious is instantly reactive to everything that happens to you in your outer world, if you accept it with your conscious mind. Never forget: whatever you take in, your mental picture of each experience, is stored in your subconscious. That's why I have warned you, again and again, to beware of using your TNT the wrong way. Learn to control your wrong reactions to the things that happen to you. Don't keep on passing to your subconscious mind fear and worry thoughts about conditions and circumstances around you. If you do, you are simply ordering that power within to keep on attracting unfavorable things to you because that is all you are picturing for it. You are creating the pattern, over and over, of what has already happened, by so doing. Your subconscious *is* infallible in its following of whatever instructions you give it with your conscious mind. It possesses an intelligent awareness but it has no reasoning power. So don't depend on your subconscious to do your thinking for you. It can *perceive* for you, if you direct it so to do, and bring you knowledge of things you need to know about, or put you in touch with sources for such knowledge . . . but it is subservient, at all times, to your desires, your decisions, your free-will choices.

You say, "think the other fellow is a nice, decent man and he will become friendly." But suppose you know definitely he is a scoundrel and a blackguard. Do you recommend one should still deceive himself in such a case?

I certainly do not recommend self-deception. If you know a certain person is "no good," as you imply, and not worthy of trust, you should, of course, be on your guard in any relations or contacts with him. Too often, however, individuals have made mistakes of a social or personal or criminal nature and have been so condemned by a self-righteous society that they are not permitted to make atonement for these mistakes. We expect ill from them, and we get what we expect. Defensively and defiantly, these people show us their worst sides because we bring this worst side out by our own attitudes. It never hurts to give any individual the "benefit of the doubt," to appeal to his or her "best side," to give him credit for the good you see in him. Since like always attracts like, if a person feels that you are sincere, if you demonstrate your faith in him, it is more than likely he will attempt to justify this faith by returning good to you.

Picture yourself being protected from the wrong thinking or wrongdoings of others. Don't let yourself fear that others will take advantage of you, because this very fear will make you susceptible. Many times people have said to me, "I can't understand what you see in So-and-So" or "How can you get along with So-and-So?" It's simply because I look for the good, while these other people put up barriers which are resented. Consequently, they awaken wrong reactions in individuals who would treat them differently if they themselves were treated differently. Even a dog can instinctively tell how you really feel about him, however much you pretend otherwise. Wouldn't you treat human beings better than dogs? If we deny others a chance to make a comeback, what hope is there for us?

I believe you said, somewhere, that a person with a work-able idea, and thoroughly convinced of its soundness, seldom has any difficulty in getting money to finance it. And yet, how many inventors, deeply convinced of the value of their inventions, have died in the poorhouse?

I have decried and denounced the unwillingness of many scientists and other intelligent people to accept or even consider *new* ideas. With regard to *telepathy*, I have stated that practically all the great electrical scientists, including Edison, Steinmetz, Tesla and Marconi, were greatly interested in telepathy. So was Dr. Alexis Carrel, who believed in it and declared that a study should be made of it by scientific men, just as physiological phenomena are studied. But despite this interest and the investigations of scientists like Dr. J. B. Rhine at Duke University, the London Society for Psychical Research, the American Society and others, there are still scientists who belittle this work. They do not wish to consider *any* idea which might upset their already-established theories. It is this "closed mind" attitude which the average inventor encounters. An inventor is often a quiet, introspective individual who has not had too much experience in facing the world. He can *visualize* what he desires to invent with faith and confidence that the creative power within will help produce it for him, but he cannot visualize with equal faith and confidence the gaining of recognition and resources for his invention. This, to him, is a different world. He submits his invention to a few prospects, and if he is rebuffed, he often becomes discouraged, even despondent, and pictures failure.

Under these conditions, the inventor is working the creative power against himself. Because you are a "successful visualizer" in one phase of your life activity is no indication that you can be or are equally successful in other phases. The same right thinking must apply to all and any of your desires or needs. Some men and women naturally possess what is called a "money consciousness"—they *see* themselves making money, everything they touch turning to money—and the power within helps them make and attract money. But many of these same people are just as unsuccessful in other departments of their lives, as is evidenced by ill health, inability to get along with others, lack of personal happiness and contentment and all kinds of other deficiencies.

Each inventor should face his problem of selling and marketing his invention, of getting financing for it, with the same enthusiasm, the same persistence, the same energetic application of his visualizing powers that he has given to the development and creation of the invention itself. If he does, he will certainly succeed in his enterprise, as any and all succeed who make proper use of "that someth' .o" within.

How can we distinguish real hunches as opposed to our mere wishful thinking, the expression of desires and passions of our conscious mind, at a given moment?

This ability to discriminate between a real hunch and an intuitive flash or premonition comes with practice. True hunches enter the conscious field of your mind without any reflection or premeditation. You just suddenly "know" or "feel" something, you get a strong urge to do or not to do something, to be on your guard, to check or investigate. Self-analysis will help you determine whether or not an impulse which you receive has been created by you through wishful thinking—an excessive desire or passion, as you characterize it. You should know yourself well enough to assume an impersonal attitude and say: "I'm just kidding myself. I wanted to get that kind of an impression, and I've stimulated my imagination to give it to me. I don't recognize this as a true hunch. My fears have dramatized themselves and given me the false feeling that something is going to happen." You will soon detect a difference in *feeling*, when a real hunch hits you.

Your remembrance of how you felt when you got this real hunch will enable you to recognize other genuine intuitive flashes and to disregard such other feelings that originate as a result of your own fears or pampered desires. You must *believe* that your inner mind can and will serve you by giving you intuitive flashes, as needed, or else the power within cannot function in this manner for you. Some people say, "I don't believe in hunches—and I've never had any, that I recall." This mental attitude has blocked off such intuitive impulses as might have been received. Learn to control your own excessive desires, things you know are not good for you, eliminate your fears, and you will then put up less and less resistance to your own reception and recognition of guidance and protection from your faculty of intuition.

My problem is not in the form of money, business or gaining fame. I have the problem of stuttering and stammering; it is foremost in my mind. Since studying your philosophy, I have noticed some improvement in my speech. I realize that results in conditions like this do not come overnight, although I would like to have rather fast results. Could you give me any hints as to how to hasten the subconscious in its wonderful work on my problem?

Go back in your life to the time, if you can recall it, when you started stuttering. What emotional experience brought on this condition? Were you criticized at a particularly sensitive moment by your parents or by someone else? Was there a dominant member of your family who repressed you, in whose presence you were afraid to express yourself? Did you feel overshadowed by someone, or did

246

you suffer such a fright that you temporarily found it impossible to speak? Somewhere in your past is the original cause of your present difficulty. Find it, and you can then release yourself from the hold this emotional reaction has had upon you. As a further aid, since stuttering and stammering are usually associated with a degree of self-consciousness and overanxiety . . . wait a few seconds before speaking. Take a breath, and *picture* in your mind what you are going to say before putting it into words. If you are groping in your mind for words, your full attention is distracted from your speech centers and, as a result, your speech is halting and sometimes broken. Recovering your ability to articulate each word correctly is largely a matter of proper "timing" and visualization. Coordinate the two, and you will soon overcome this condition.

I firmly believe in your teachings. You state that one should use this power for good and not evil. This I believe 100 percent, so that is why I am asking, would it be evil to use this power for gambling? I'm not a professional gambler, but like many people, I gamble to some extent. Would it be harmful to use this power for gambling on either a large or small scale?

Frederick Marion, noted seer and author of the book *In My Mind's Eye,* in which he tells of many of his experiences with extrasensory perception, his developed ability to sense the thoughts of others and to foresee the future, also tells of his attempts to use his powers for determining when to buy and sell stocks. For a time he was successful, then his powers commenced to fail him. He could not control his human desire to try to force an answer when so much money was riding on every hunch that he needed to "guess right." Every gambler who has used his intuition has had it fail him under pressure. Most gamblers I have known have died "broke" or have had many more downs than ups. They never knew when to stop—a success eggs them on to new losses. If they played the "game of life" straight, without tension and strain, their intuitive faculties would serve them more regularly and dependably. Life, in a sense, is a gamble—you are betting on yourself to win—and I would rather bet on myself than on a wheel of chance any day. Gambling is evil when you hurt yourself and others by doing it. Only those who can afford to lose should gamble. Unhappily, most who gamble cannot afford to lose. What is your classification? Why not bet on yourself instead? The risks are less and the gains, over a lifetime, are much greater and more satisfying.

Can you suggest a formula or plan to aid me in sorting out the best for me of several things I could do and want to do commercially?

No one can really do this for you but yourself. In your periods of meditation, say to your inner mind, the creative power within: "Determine for me wherein my best business opportunities lie—what abilities and past experiences I can crystallize and capitalize upon in my future." Give this picture to your subconscious, and then go about your business in the faith and confidence that at the right time, through an intuitive flash or a sudden awareness, you will *know* the direction in which to go and how to go about it. You can depend upon it. The answer will be forthcoming.

Some writers claim that you do not learn by experience. Please explain what you mean by "learning by experience."

Learning by experience how *not* to do things as well as how to do them. Learning to profit by the experiences of others. Why should you make the same mistakes others have made if you observe in advance that a path they have taken has led them up a "dead-end street"? Use your intelligence as well as your faith in facing life and its problems.

I am stymied or bogged down with "clutter-clutter." How can I get out from under the feeling of chaos?

By eliminating your confused and disturbed thinking. You have formed the bad habit of paying too much attention to little, unimportant, insignificant details and happenings, building them up into mountains and obstacles in your mind. They thus have become, as you have described, a lot of "clutter-clutter," milling around in your conscious mind, obstructing real thoughts and ideas that are trying to get through to you. You have a constant feeling of impending chaos only because these disturbed thoughts give you the sensation of being overwhelmed or engulfed by them. Throw them out, through an act of will and it will be "good-bye, chaos—welcome law and order" in your mind.

What place does imagination have in the scheme of things if it is liable to mislead one's thinking?

Right direction of imagination, like anything else, makes it a tremendous power for good instead of harm. Imagine good things coming to you, and good eventually comes as you have pictured it, through imagination; imagine ill, and you will get bad results in due time.

What is imagination?

Imagination is that faculty of mind which enables you to form in your inner consciousness a mental image or picture of what you want. It is the stimulator of thought, the activator of the creative power within, the means of making your desires specific.

How do you picture or think of the God Power or Presence within when you pray? Can you just pray to a feeling of inner power?

Each person has his own concepts of God, and whatever concept that is most satisfying, meaningful and helpful to you is the one you should use in your meditations and prayers. I certainly do not picture God, when I pray, as anthropomorphic in nature, seated on some vast throne somewhere in heavenly space. I have long since outgrown this childhood concept. Today, I have the conviction that a part of God, the Great Intelligence, indwells each human soul—yours and mine. You can recall how close you have felt and still feel toward a loved one. As you think of that loved one *now*, you bring him or her instantly to mind, and you feel the bond of closeness which exists. In much the same way, let these feelings of closeness and intimacy come to you from God. You know your loved one exists as you think of him or her; you haven't the slightest doubt about it. Then, let yourself feel and know that God exists, and you will sense the God Presence within—the power that will never let you down, to which you can go in meditation and prayer and from which you may expect right answers.

Would you kindly tell me what techniques one may use to blot out unhappy experiences of the past, and how to forgive one's loved ones?

By realizing that you are doing yourself great harm by retaining the bitter memory of these experiences—that you are not hurting those who have hurt you nearly as much as you are hurting yourself. Review what has happened in your mind, then *picture* in your mind's eye what you now realize you should have said and done. Assume your share of the blame and responsibility and, however justified you may feel for holding malice against your loved ones, *let go* now

250

of all your hate and resentment. Know and believe that the law of compensation will take care of them, eventually, for their misdeeds and wrong thinking. Realize that as long as your attention is fixed on the past and its unhappiness and on losses you can never recover, you are holding yourself back from receiving new resources, new opportunities and new experiences of a happy nature. Remember, like attracts like, and you have been attracting a repetition of miserable feelings as you have lived these experiences over and over. It isn't worth it. It will destroy all health and happiness in time, unless abandoned—and unless a new, positive attitude is assumed.

Is there a difference between prayer and meditation?

Yes. Meditation is preparation for prayer, through relaxing the physical body of all tension, making the conscious mind passive and then, with your attention turned inward, entering upon prayerful visualization of those things you need and desire.

If your parents keep reminding you from childhood to adulthood that you cannot succeed, how can you remove this block successfully?

This is a fine heritage for parents to pass on to a child into adulthood—a series of "you can't succeed" pictures! Your first step toward the liberation of your consciousness from this parental bondage is the realization that the moment you reject their negative concepts of you, these wrong pictures can no longer retain their hold over your mind. You have to *believe* that you can't succeed before you will fail. Put out of your mind all resentment of what your father and mother have done to you. As long as you remain bitter, you will keep these unhappy pictures and their influence alive in your consciousness. Let go of this bitterness, and these pictures will be deprived of all nourishment in mind and die of starvation. There is much remaining in life for you that is good and worthwhile. Claim it through right visualization and the exercise of faith in yourself and in the unfailing power of "that something" to bring you what you have long desired and deserved!

Let me determine if I understand you: you form the picture of your desire, consciously, and then, while being very quiet, it is reflected back to you, probably only for the fraction of a second! Is this reflection what you mean by "seeing it in your mind's eye"? And is this what must happen, before the creative power within can be impelled to bring you effective results?

Yes, you have described the process very well. You first create the mental image of what you desire, and then project it upon the inner mental screen through an act of will, letting yourself feel a strong desire for the materialization of this picture in real life, having faith, at the same time, that what you have visualized has already been achieved in mind and is even now on the way to you!

With the world in such a turmoil, how can a person keep free of worry and fear? How can the unpleasant happenings be kept out of mind?

By refusing to personalize those happenings that have no direct relation to you. Recognize that fear and worry will not correct the world situation, nor even help you solve any of your own problems. In fact, fear and worry are demoralizing and devitalizing. In time, they can destroy self-confidence, health and happiness. Realize that you yourself are reasonably well and happy *now*, and that your greatest contribution to yourself and others will always be the maintenance of a positive, cheerful, optimistic attitude. Stop living in a "hope for the best and fear the worst" state of mind. The worst hardly ever happens, and when you aim at the best, things always turn out better than you have thought possible.

What is the quickest way to relax?

I presume the quickest way would be to hit yourself on the head with a hammer, but the after-effects wouldn't be too desirable. The next quickest, but safe and sane, way is to get off by yourself, if possible, sit down in an easy chair or stretch out on a cot, and *let go* of your physical body with your conscious mind—lift arms and legs and drop them, let the chair or bed support your entire body. You will feel a lightness and sense of buoyancy come over you. Then, with your body relaxed, let go of all feelings of mental tension brought about by high pressure, fear, worry or other emotional disturbances. Visualize a blank mental screen, a quiet pool of water, a calm, restful landscape—anything which suggests a peaceful, motionless area. The instant you have done this, you are relaxed; it should take you less than two minutes, with practice, to let go in this manner.

Can you induce dreams by suggestion and cause your intuition to make known certain information to you in this way?

Yes, much knowledge can be revealed to you through dreams, and the creative power within often uses a dream as a medium through which to present information you need to have of past, present or future events. Of course, the difficulty of correct interpretation often enters in because many dreams are caused by disturbed physical and mental states (such as indigestion, fear, worry, suspicion or resentment). There is a tendency, when the conscious mind is made passive through sleep, for the troubles of the day to dramatize themselves in distorted dream form, and this type of dream is seldom significant. It may reveal to the psychiatrist the causes of your fears, apprehensions and other emotional instabilities, but little or nothing to you. However, there are other times when you are projected ahead into the future, and your intuitive faculties bring you vivid dreams, in whole or in part, of events coming toward you in time—events for which the causes already exist, causes you may have set up in yourself through your reaction to past experiences. These dreams deserve your most careful analysis, for they may give you a clue as to how you should prepare to meet or to avoid a developing situation. These dream warnings, properly evaluated, can enable you to change your thinking and thus change the possible happenings themselves.

Upon retiring, if you desire an answer, during sleep, to a pressing problem, suggest to "that something" within that it bring you the answer in this manner. With practice, you can often induce the reception of information you need, in dreams. Many people say: "I decided to sleep on it, and I woke up with the answer!"

Just recently I have been plagued by the feeling that people are criticizing me behind my back or saying unkind things about me. This feeling is making me nervous and self-conscious. Do you know what has caused me to react this way? It's not at all like me, and it frightens me.

You are extremely sensitive by nature. Check back in your life and see if you haven't had an experience wherein someone thoughtlessly made an unkind or critical remark in a moment of misunderstanding or temper. Such a remark may have been such a shock to you that it left a "psychic scar." Ever since then you may have become growingly apprehensive that some other friends or relatives would be criticizing you, until now you fear everyone may be viewing you in a critical light. This would naturally make you self-conscious and apprehensive. Or perhaps you have become overly conscientious, trying to attain something worthwhile in life, and subconsciously feel you are not quite equal to it. You may fear others will recognize this fact and start saying behind your back, "She thinks she's somebody but she really isn't"—and so on. Are you actually battling a growing sense of inferiority? Whatever the cause, get quietly off by yourself and try to "see yourself as others *really* see you," not as you *imagine* they see you. This self-analysis should disclose your weaknesses and enable you to take a new mental attitude that will help overcome your feelings. The chances are there is little basis in fact for your nervous apprehensions.

You have said one can get anything he desires in life, provided he works hard enough for it and visualizes what he wants correctly. Well, I've been trying but so far have gotten lots of things I don't want—and I'm afraid I'm never going to get what I really wish to have. How do you explain this?

I have said: "You can attain whatever you desire in life, within the range of your capabilities, if you put forth the proper effort and visualize clearly what you wish to achieve." You have not stated what your goal in life is, but anything worthwhile can rarely be attained overnight, unless you are almost ready for its realization. In many instances, what you desire may require the acquisition of experience and ability before you possess what it takes to reach your objective. If, while you are striving toward a goal, your fears and worries cause you to picture failure instead of success, you will most certainly attract many things you haven't wanted. Remember—this God-given creative power within your subconscious mind is subject to the direction of your conscious mind. Whatever you picture becomes an order to the subconscious, and this creative power, as I have said, acts like a magnet in trying to produce what you have pictured in your actual life. This means you must learn how to control your thinking, how to rule out your fear and worry thoughts, how to keep on picturing, confidently and vividly, what you desire to be or have or attain. The more earnestly and persistently you continue this visualization, the nearer you will be brought to the goal you have set for yourself. This takes practice, patience and endurance, but it always pays off.

If man is master of his fate, responsible to no one but himself, how can you resolve this and the fact that life has been at work in a thousand ways, functioning as a "going concern" before he was born? It certainly appears that, at every point, we are involved in processes, functions and activities over which we are unable to exercise any significant control. How do you answer this?

Man *should* be master of his fate. He was so designed and given the potentiality through a creative power within, capable of carrying him to inconceivable heights. But en masse, man thus far has not made too intelligent use of this power. Individually, however, man's achievements have approached the sublime.

Give a thought to Steinmetz, the electrical wizard, who was born with a misshapen head, a hunchback, spindly legs, an over-all frail body. Those who knew Steinmetz say that they lost all consciousness of his body—the brilliance of the man caused it to fade from sight. Surely, he was "master of his fate."

Think, too, of Beethoven, whom nature endowed with an ugly face and a defect which should have been fatal to anyone who aspired to write music—he became deaf! And yet the mind of Beethoven brought forth some of the noblest music ever written, music that will live forever and bring joy to millions still unborn. Few human beings realize, when they thrill to Beethoven's greatest work, his *Ninth Symphony*, that this great composer never heard a single note of it!

The list of those who have been "master of their individual fates" is endless. Hundreds and thousands of men and women, calling upon "that something"—the creative power within—have surmounted all the "processes, functions and activities" which they found in existence when they arrived here, and which ordinarily might have been thought to be against them, obstacles to their attainment of any success!

No. Man has not been cast adrift in this world, a victim of circumstances and forces beyond his control. He possesses in his inner consciousness all the power he needs for *self-mastery*. Man has been endowed with this power from birth by the incomprehensibly great Creator. He has but to discover it and learn to use it. That is all.

THOUGHTS TO BUILD INTO YOUR LIFE

I have many questions I would like to ask about the HOW and WHY of things.

I realize, however, that the answer to these questions can be found in my own subconscious, if I impress my inner mind with the prayerful desire to be shown the right way to do things.

The sooner I can learn to rely upon guidance and protection from the power of God, the sooner will I be independent—able to stand on my own feet.

I know that so long as I do not release hate and resentment and prejudice from my consciousness that I cannot become aware of the presence of God.

To be master of my fate, I must develop mental and emotional control which, in turn, raises the rate and character of my vibrations and attracts better and better things to me.

20

Share Your Good Fortune with Others

When you get hold of a good thing, pass it on. That's the way to win friends and attract more people to you. Don't be selfish. When you get the opportunity, help others to understand TNT and to make it do the same for them that it has done for you. Every time you give others a lift, you give yourself a bigger one.

Some people, who don't understand and don't want to understand, may say you are conceited, self-centered, or selfish; but don't let this disturb you. Those are the scoffers . . . those who would put rocks in your road and otherwise impede your progress. You'll always encounter this type on the highways and byways of life. They are not going anywhere and want to take you along with them. Those who understand will want what you have to give them and will be helpful, eager to serve you, to work with you. The intelligent ones, as they observe the headway you are making, will begin to study you to determine what you have that they haven't and to try to discover your secret.

I have given you a grip on it; hold to it tightly and start moving forward.

You won't have to batter others down to get where you want to go; you won't have to climb over their dead bodies; you won't have to doublecross your friends and business associates; you won't have to reach your goal through connivance and pretense and deceit. You'll get there with your head up and your feet firmly on the ground. And what you have been able to do once, you'll know how to do again and again, and do better each time.

This is what the creative power of mind, working in and through you, can and will do for you. As you progress, you will find that you'll wish to do charitable things, good things, for other people—perform services, little acts of kindness and thoughtfulness, go an extra mile or two to help the other fellow when you can, in appreciation of what has been done for you. As and when you do this, you'll observe that your friendly acts will bring about a willingness in the other fellow to do something for you. There is nothing selfish about this—it's just a matter of cause and effect.

André Ampère knew the law. He called it the law of attraction as applied to electrical magnetism. *"Parallel currents in the same direction attract one another."* Simple, isn't it? And when you are out of tune and antagonistic, you put others out of tune and make them antagonistic because: *"Parallel currents in opposite directions repel one another."* It's the old, old true story boiled down to three big little words: *Like begets like!*

When you perform a service you will be paid huge dividends. There is no mystery about it, it's just so!

Start doing what you've been told to do, over and over again, until your technique of right thinking is perfected.

There is strength in teamwork. Get others in on this kind of thinking with you! Working together will inspire more enthusiasm, confidence and determination for each of you to keep making progress.

If you accept what I am telling you in the spirit in which it is given and put it into execution, you will be unbeatable. And by getting in tune and getting others on the track, the world is yours!

When Fear rules the will, nothing can be done, but when a man casts Fear out of his mind, the world becomes his oyster.

To lose a bit of money is nothing, but to lose hope—to lose nerve and ambition—that is what makes men cripples.

Herbert N. Casson

Charles M. Schwab once said: "Many of us think of salesmen as people traveling around with sample kits. Instead, we are all salesmen, every day of our lives. We are selling our ideas, our plans, our energies, our enthusiasm to those with whom we come in contact."

So it is with every endeavor, and especially is this true of selling commodities, because there you *must* contact people.

And when I say "contact," I mean contacting them face-to-face. The day of order-taking is once more disappearing. It really never was here, because there is no substitute for seeing prospects face to face. But even more in the days to come, the only persons who will achieve outstanding success will be those who get out and "beat the bushes" and meet people. The others will be left far behind.

You cannot get around the fundamental law of "survival of the fittest." Therefore, forget about order-taking and keep in mind the only way you can close a sale is to *make the prospect think as you think!* The best way will always be face-to-face contact. You have *got* to be in his presence, you have *got* to see his reactions—"the old law of cause and effect"—and you have *got* to adapt yourself to the varying conditions that confront you with the individual prospects.

If you are intent on making a sale (and you must be if you are going to succeed), keep in mind my theme. The subconscious mind will be giving you ideas, hunches, inspirations—a perfect flood of them—that will guide you correctly. They will point the way to get into a busy man's presence, into the privacy of his very self, and when you get there, to stand on both feet.

261

Be alert. Make your prospect feel your personality. Know what you are talking about. Be enthusiastic. Don't quail!

You are just as good as he is, and besides, you may have something which he hasn't, and that is utmost confidence, utmost faith in the article you are selling. On the other hand, if he is a success, he also has personality. Therefore, be sure to put the contact on a fifty-fifty basis. Do not belittle him; do not let him belittle you. Meet on common ground. Make him like you, and when he likes *you* and you *him,* success is on its way. Hold in mind from the start that you are going to sell him. . . . *You are going to sell him!*

Your main, all-over theme in life, of course, is: "*I am going to succeed in everything I undertake . . . I am going to succeed in everything I undertake!* (Repetition, reiteration, repeating, repeating, seeing yourself doing it, over and over, visualizing, "I can! . . . I will! . . . I believe it—and it is so!")

Get your friends interested. Form study groups. Exchange experiences. Discuss your failures. Find out what mistakes you made. The reasons for them. Pick up the pieces and try again. Criticize each other. Determine why certain plans didn't work out. Share the news and the joy of your successes! Conduct experiments in telepathy, in developing your powers of visualization, concentration, intuition. Demonstrate the value of TNT to your friends, family and business associates, as their interest in this power develops.

With a nucleus of interest in TNT eventually established in each community, with large numbers of men and women studying and applying the power of right thinking, great changes will begin to take place in the minds and hearts of people and the world!

Each owner of this book can set up his own center and start to work with his own interested friends and associates. The secret is all here . . . ready to be unfolded to each reader, each student.

It helps your development to work with an understanding friend or loved one. It gives you added impetus. You can check, assist and encourage each other. The more you talk about inner power of mind, the more thought and study you give to it, the more it becomes manifest in your life.

Keep at it, never let up, never give up, because the answer exists for the solution of every problem you have had or could have in *your own mind!*

And remember, always, to share your good fortune with others. You will be rewarded a hundredfold . . . a thousand . . . as your sharing continues, because good compounds itself—multiplies, keeps on multiplying, expanding, returning more and more good to the original giver.

Once more let me assure you—you *can* be what you want, provided you are willing to pay the price in time, thought, effort and energy. You now have the KEY. It is up to you to unlock these higher powers of mind and make them work!

Throw out all *negative* thoughts . . .
Assume and maintain a POSITIVE mental attitude . . .
SAY to yourself:
I've got TNT . . .
I've got the POWER OF DECISION . . .
I've got the VOICE WITHIN . . .
I've got a CREATIVE POWER IN MY MIND . . .
I've got FAITH in MYSELF and the POWER OF GOD in me . . .
I'm going to USE these POWERS so I can bring GOOD THINGS to pass in my life NOW!

Persevere!
Have faith!
Visualize!
YOU CAN'T MISS!

THOUGHTS TO BUILD INTO YOUR LIFE

In appreciation of all the good I have gained and am gaining from my use of TNT, I am passing on the knowledge of it to my friends and loved ones—every person who expresses a desire for self-betterment.

I know that no one can benefit from the use of TNT until and unless he or she wants to learn about it.

I know, too, that the best way for me to call this highly productive power of TNT to the attention of anyone is to keep on demonstrating it successfully in my own life.

My theme in life now is: "I'm going to succeed in everything I undertake!"

I am going to repeat this declaration, time and again, giving thanks to God for that which has already been achieved.

I am resolved to persevere, to have faith, to visualize and I know that, if I do these things, that I can't fail. Things, eventually *must* turn out right!

21

Your TNT for Today

This book will do everything for you that is claimed, but you must reread it and reread it until every sentence, every word is thoroughly understood; and then you must apply the principles and mechanics with your whole heart and soul. Make them a part of your daily life and when you put into practice the ideas offered, you will find that they will work just as they've always worked and always will. If you are in deadly earnest with yourself, you will find the entire scheme very simple.

After you have studied the book and have reflected upon the ideas set forth, you will appreciate the tremendous force which lies in the science of *thought repetition* and *positive action*.

You can, by repetition of the same thought, push yourself upward or downward, depending on whether you have depressed or constructive thoughts. And as you build yourself powerfully, you will find that you can influence others by your thoughts.

Therefore, let me again admonish you to exercise great care that you do not misuse your power. Keep your mind filled with good, constructive thoughts, and then act with all the energy you possess as the ideas come to you.

Stop looking backward. You know where you've been; you want to know where you are *going!* Train your mind's eye on the future! This is the glorious land in which your opportunities lie. Gradually, as you become more and more adept in the control and direction of "that something," the creative power within, your intuition will bring you glimpses of your future.

You are not in this world alone; you are here to help others even as you will be helped. You are important to yourself, to your friends and loved ones, to your community, your nation. What you are doing in life is important. The work of every individual counts in the great scheme of things. No good effort is ever lost.

James Russell Lowell said:

> No man is born into the world whose work
> Is not born with him; there is always work
> And tools to work withal, for those who will,
> And blessed are the horny hands of toil. . . .

When you do the best you can each day, whatever your job or responsibility may be, you are improving yourself and the conditions around you.

Knowing that you possess this power within, and knowing how to draw upon it, you need not waste your time and energy worrying about national and international conditions which are beyond your influence.

Make your influence felt where you live, and you will be doing your part and inspiring others to do theirs.

Remember, *every thought, kept ever constant, leads to action, and results follow.*

So keep this book always close at hand. Reread it, study it, and reread and study it as frequently as possible.

Practice, practice, practice! Inspire others by your daily demonstration of right thinking!

To aid you in this practice, I have prepared *100 Powerful Affirmations* for you to make a part of your *Personal Progress Program*.

If you like, you can print these individual declarations on cards. Then, each day, select whatever affirmation applies to your specific needs. Put this card on your mirror or some place where you can glance at it occasionally—or carry it with you in your pocket so you can look at it in spare moments.

Keep this affirmation uppermost in your mind during the day. Get it in your consciousness. There are a sufficient number of *Powerful Affirmations* for you to shuffle the cards and take one at random, if you prefer this method, as your *day's assignment*.

OR, you can take the thoughts in succession, from 1 to 100, and then work through them again, when your 100-Day Program is finished, because they each are POWER UNITS which, once built into your mind, keep on increasing your charge of TNT!

So . . . here is the POWER within YOU—in capsule, everyday form:

1. I am completely relaxed in body and mind.
2. I see myself as a magnet, attracting all good things to me.
3. I am filled with an inner feeling of quiet calm, assurance and security.
4. I am finishing whatever I start, to the best of my ability.
5. I am putting forth my best effort to discover and develop what I am best fitted to do.
6. I am picturing, at all times, only good things coming to me.
7. I have faith in myself and the creative power within me.
8. Knowing that I have the power within to solve all my problems, I am facing the future with supreme confidence.

9. I am serving my fellow man as best I can, knowing that he, in his way, is serving me.

10. I am serving others in the knowledge and faith that the great law of life is *giving*, and the great reward for *giving* is *receiving*.

11. By steadfastly holding in mind the same picture of what I desire, I know I am attracting what I need in resources and experiences to make this picture come true in my life.

12. I am eliminating, as best I can, all fear and worry thoughts from my consciousness.

13. I am doing my best to undo mistakes of the past and am resolved I will not make such mistakes again.

14. I am releasing all feelings of hate and resentment against others in the realization that they are more damaging to me than to them.

15. I am doing everything possible to make up to others for any wrongs I now realize I have done to them.

16. I am forgiving others for their misdeeds against me, so that my mind may be freed of bitter feelings and concentrated upon happier, more worthwhile things.

17. I know that what I am picturing cannot be denied me, as long as I am willing to put forth the necessary effort to get it.

18. I am clearing my consciousness of all past wrong thoughts and feelings so that I can replace them with right thoughts and feelings.

19. I am analyzing my past actions impersonally, in order that I may discover and remove any faults in myself which might otherwise prove injurious.

20. I refuse, from this moment on, to let fear dominate any part of my life.

21. I am picturing myself facing similar situations today as I now realize I should have faced them in the past.

22. I am rooting out old fears from my consciousness and

creating new thought and habit patterns of courage and resolution which will enable me to face any future test or emergency as it should be met.

23. To constantly remind myself that fear is just a state of mind, I am repeating this declaration every time fear seeks to control me: "Fear knocked at the door—Faith opened it—and there was NOTHING there!"

24. I have faith that I can always call upon the creative power within for help, guidance and protection.

25. I am assuming full responsibility for my thoughts and acts.

26. I am giving my creative power of mind definite orders of what I want it to do for me.

27. I am correcting any decisions I have made which I discover to have been wrong.

28. I am keeping abreast of the times so that I can take advantage of the opportunities which surround me.

29. I am ruling by body as well as my mind, knowing that moderation in all things is the safe rule of life to follow.

30. I am protecting myself from the destructive thoughts of others by holding my own thoughts and emotions under control.

31. I have the intestinal fortitude and resolution to make up my mind as important issues, demanding the right decisions, arise.

32. I am not permitting excessive feelings of anger, fear, excitement and the like to take possession of me and upset the chemistry of my body.

33. As a daily aid to health, I am observing moderation and regular habits in eating, drinking, working, playing and sleeping.

34. I am repeating my mental picture of perfect health, day after day, as often as needed, to keep this healing faculty of mind actively busy and intensely on the job repairing and re-creating my body.

35. I am concentrating on such specific organs of my body as may require special *picturizing* attention in the matter of health.

36. I am seeing myself protected from all forms of disease, infection and injury, through guidance of my creative and intuitive powers within.

37. I am daily repeating this vitalizing affirmation: "I am and will continue to be well and happy, physically and mentally."

38. I am prepared to adapt myself agreeably to all those who differ from me in temperament, mental outlook and emotional nature, as well as in religion, race and politics.

39. I am constantly reminding myself that the only way to enjoy friendly relations with people of all races, colors and creeds is to always: "Judge the individual—and not the race, color or creed."

40. I am, without prejudice or favor, giving every person the benefit of the doubt in any situation or association until and if he proves by his conduct or attitude that he does not rate such consideration.

41. As a means of improving my personal relations with friends and loved ones, I am now demagnetizing myself from the memory of all past, unhappy experiences I have had with them.

42. I am mindful of the fact that what I have not overcome in myself I cannot help overcome in others.

43. I am keeping always in mind that, to get along with others, I must be tolerant, understanding and forgiving of their shortcomings, as I would wish them to be of mine.

44. I am, from now on, resolved to do with my life what my inner self tells me that I can and should be doing, without interference, willful or otherwise, from any other human being.

45. I am not permitting anyone, from this moment on, to dominate me, economically or personally, nor I, them —since I know that such domination, either way, is weakening to both.

46. I am proceeding courageously and persistently in everything I do.

47. I am sticking to any decision I make until the job or task I have decided upon is accomplished.

48. I am picturing only good things happening—expecting only good.

49. I am beginning, at once, to plan a logical, definite way of working myself out of any dominating situation I may be in.

50. I am no longer accepting domination from a father or mother, or other relative or friend.

51. I am accepting my responsibility for the care of relatives who need care, at the same time insisting that other relatives assume their share of this responsibility, so any burdens will be evenly divided and as cheerfully borne as possible.

52. I am releasing any relatives or friends from any and all feelings of obligation to me which have denied them their right to freedom.

53. I am assuming an attitude toward all others to whom I feel obligated, or who may feel themselves obligated to me, that: "To be free myself—I must first let others be free.

54. I am free and independent, in complete possession of my free will and free choice, capable of deciding in my mind and heart what I want most to do or be or have.

55. I am always keeping in mind that the power to love, properly expressed by me in life, is indispensable if I would enjoy genuine happiness, health and prosperity.

56. I am giving first attention to the finer expression of love in all my life activities and associations.

57. I know that I must love to be loved, to be happy, to be balanced physically, mentally and emotionally.

58. I am respecting the rights and interests of my married partner, remembering that this is a fifty-fifty relationship, and that the giving and receiving of love is the foundation of it.

59. I am constantly picturing a life of love and happiness (married or single), for I know that love is the greatest, most wonderful, most vitalizing force in the universe—that love is actually life itself!

60. I am equal in personality expression to anyone else because I have an equal degree of creative power in mind to draw upon—in the fuller and fuller expression of my personality.

61. I am overcoming all fears which have been preventing and retarding the full expression of my personality.

62. I possess poise, the ability to be composed and at ease, in the presence of others.

63. I am making every effort to become a more understanding, appealing personality and to overcome all feelings of self-consciousness, inferiority, shyness and timidity.

64. I am no longer comparing myself unfavorably with others.

65. I am expressing myself freely and assuredly when on my feet in public.

66. I am giving daily attention to the kind of dress and personal hygiene which I know will improve my appearance.

67. I am assuming an optimistic, cheerful point of view under any and all conditions as the best attitude to maintain in overcoming difficulties.

68. I am taking a sincere interest in other people and their activities, realizing that interest in others begets interest in me and my work, in return.

69. I am stepping out of my shell—putting myself more in circulation, so that I can constantly meet and make new friends.

70. I am offering my services to others when I see I may be of genuine help.

71. I am resolved to be my natural, sincere self, to avoid temptation to be a show-off, or to boast of my accomplishments.

72. I am removing from my mind all fears of limitation, lack of money, poverty and the like, so that there is nothing in consciousness to attract economic loss to me.

73. I am picturing myself earning and receiving the money I need, and attracting either a new position, a raise or the opportunity to make this money through other sources.

74. I am making it a habit to move in circles where there are people with money-making possibilities in need of my special talents and services.

75. I am picturing everything as well with me financially, and I have faith that all will be well.

76. I am picturing myself as rich in possibilities and opportunities which I can and will convert into money.

77. I am putting forth every effort to develop talents and skills which I must have in exchange for money.

78. I am picturing money coming to mé from every good source, in answer to my needs and desires.

79. I am taking this moment to picture whatever I want to do or be or have in life, letting myself feel that it has already been achieved in mind, so that my creative power may have this picture as a blueprint from which to work.

80. I am imagining a blank, white motion picture screen, stretched across the dark room of my inner mind—or letting myself *feel* that such a screen is there, as a

273

focal point of attention, so that I can throw the picture of what I want upon it.

81. Having pictured what I want, I am going about the daily business of living, putting forth every effort in the direction pictured, with the supreme faith and confidence that I will be led by my creative power within to take the right steps to arrive, eventually, at my visualized objective.

82. I realize that my subconscious mind, having no limitation as to time and space, can reach out and make connection with all the elements and people I need, to help make what I picture come true.

83. I have confidence in myself and my ability to work with the creative power within me.

84. I have confidence in the goals in life I have pictured for myself.

85. I have confidence that I can face difficult problems and work out the right solution.

86. I have confidence that the future is mine to make of it what I will.

87. I am removing the word *can't* from my consciousness forever.

88. I am picturing myself always being in the right place at the right time, meeting the right people who have the power to place me in touch with the right opportunities, circumstances and resources, leading me to take the right action to bring me the right financial or any other kinds of results I desire.

89. I am loaded with TNT and am putting forth every effort to make full use of this creative power within me.

90. I am discarding from my consciousness all worthless thoughts as they occur or are recalled—the debris of a lifetime—and am concentrating henceforth on only the things that count, that can bring me greater happiness, health, security and peace of mind.

91. I am maintaining a positive, optimistic attitude of mind in the face of all seemingly negative conditions.
92. I am replacing my fears and worries with courage and faith.
93. I refuse to permit any setbacks to upset me as they have in the past.
94. I am picturing good things happening and am supporting these good pictures with every earnest endeavor in their behalf.
95. I know that, as I keep control of my emotions, the creative power within is guiding and protecting me.
96. I know that I can do what others have done and are doing, in overcoming obstacles and handicaps in life.
97. I have faith that, as I persevere in my positive attitude toward everything and everybody, all the happiness, health and good things in life I desire are coming to me in time.
98. I declare now that, however great the odds may seem to be against me, I am never surrendering to despair or discouragement or defeat.
99. I give thanks for the strength to meet each day, for each small victory that I gain.
100. *I now declare, having faith in myself and the Infinite Intelligence within me—that I have absolute faith in my future!*